THE STORIES
WE TELL

To Stina and Arthur
who live a very
good story.
All my love!
Ros

THE STORIES WE TELL

COMPOSING IN A DECOMPOSING WORLD

Ruth Newton

New Voices Series v. 4

Florida Academic Press
Gainesville and London

Copyright © 2006 by Florida Academic Press

All rights reserved. No part of this book may be reproduced or transmitted in any form or manner, by any means, mechanical, electronic or other including by photocopying, recording or via information storage and retrieval systems, without the express permission of Florida Academic Press, except for the inclusion of brief quotations in reviews.

Published in the United States of America by Florida Academic Press,
Gainesville, FL, July 2006
Cover and interior layout by Gordon Woolf

ISBN-10: 1-890357-18-9
ISBN-13: 978-1-890357-18-4

Library of Congress Cataloging-in-Publication Data:

Newton, Ruth, 1932-
 The stories we tell : composing in a decomposing world / Ruth Newton.
   p. cm. -- (New voices series ; v. 4)
 Includes bibliographical references.
 ISBN 1-890357-18-9
 1. Epic literature--History and criticism. 2. Fiction--History and criticism. 3. Narration
 (Rhetoric) I. Title. II. Series: New voices series (Gainesville, Fla.)
 PN56.E65N52 2006
 809.3'911--dc22
                                                   2006013271

Contents

Preface	1
Thoughts From an Epic Prison	3
The Oldest and Newest Story	3
La Ronde	5
And Death Shall Have no Distinction	10
The Myth of Progress	13
Reading the Heroic Story Poorly	15
The Public Epic	25
An Epic Loss of Will	35
An Epic Failure of Empathic Imagination	43
Sanity and Slaughter	48
How the Novel Got Its Game	53
The House of Fiction	53
Form as a Problem	60
Morality as a Problem	72
The Truth of the Story	78
The Author	82
The Characters	92
The Reader	106
Abbreviations	112
NOTES	113
Bibliography	131

Preface

THE EPIC AND THE NOVEL, a bread and butter offering to college freshmen in the days beyond recall, were solid pillars of the Humanities, or so we assumed. But time has put its mark on both genres in surprising ways.

Georg Lukács argues convincingly that the heroes of the Homeric epic lived in a world of totality[1] which was commensurate with their desires, a world of answers, not questions, of finding, not seeking. This was the world, as well, of Thucydides and his Pericles, a world in which Athenians read Homer assiduously, a world in which history and the epic flowed together harmoniously. But as the world became more problematic, the epic could no longer speak to its audience, nor could history remain its ally.

It was the novel which reached its greatest flowering at a time when history took an adversarial stand towards the story, when answers turned into questions, and choices were paramount and painful. The authors and their characters still thought in terms of totality but morality had become a problem,[2] the full scope of which remained unrecognized.

Now, in our time, bordering on chaos and the absurd, we have no trouble recognizing morality as a problem. The stories we try to tell are overwhelmed by history and the way to a transcendental home is lost. Two contradictory types of narrative answer the unravelings of such an age: a return to the epic in the form of performance art, and the development of the novel as game, with all its concomitant effects. These narratives are examined in the following pages.

Thoughts From an Epic Prison

The Oldest and Newest Story

WHAT MUST IT HAVE BEEN LIKE for those who lived in a world where, according to Georg Lukács, "life and meaning were present with perfect immanence in every manifestation of life."[1] And to have had a rich form of literature which we recognize as entirely appropriate to such an age, an age of totality in which history cooperates in such a way that Thucydides' actors, who drank the story of Hektor and Akhilleus with their mother's milk, were inspired to emulate their heroics in the Peloponnesian War, lasting 17 years longer than the Trojan War.

Though Pericles boasted that Athens had no need for a Homer, he could not do without that rhetoric of honor, long before the age of mock-heroics mimicked the hacking off of limbs and heads. And it is said that Alexander carried *The Iliad* wherever he went.

Art anticipates and invents life, Oscar Wilde wryly observes,[2] dictating not only how but what we see. And indeed, the historian Thucydides, so much closer to the Homeric epic, could not avoid the uncanny imitations history performs, despite his intense effort to separate it from myth and romance.

His own storied biography overlaps the very narrative he is presenting. He suffers the plague with the populace, leads troops into battle, loses an important encounter at Amphipolis against the skillful Spartan Brasidas. Since his country did not look kindly upon losing, (the caution of Athenian generals may have been inspired by their state's custom of execution, disgrace and banishment), he becomes an exile and adds to an insider's special discernment the objective judgments of an outsider as well. But he is careful to let history speak for itself; his moral lessons are muted, leaving us to our own discernment and conclusions. He assumes a distant stance in beginning his account, introducing himself as Thucydides, an Athenian, before sliding into "I",[3] and returning to the third person again later in the eleventh year of the war

Right out of the gate the historian hopes to offer an exact knowledge of the past, checking sources, reading monuments, cross-examining eyewitnesses, recording speeches others had heard and making notes of those to which he was witness. Since it was difficult, without transcripts, to quote any of the 141 speeches verbatim, on various occasions he says what he thinks is demanded of the speakers, "adhering as closely as possible to the general sense of what they really said."[4]

When Thucydides begins his chronicle in 431 B.C., he thinks he can enlighten future generations by making a pretty clean piece of work out of a war that would last at the most three years. Though the terrible plague, which weakened Athens severely over a long period of time, takes from the historian in 429 his most eminent character who thought the first year of outbreak "had done more than any other calamity to ruin the spirit of Athens,"[5] he nevertheless soldiers on with his recital of events until the middle of 411 BC. But the war continues until 404! No Kalkhas was around, as he had been in Book 2 of *The Iliad*, to gauge the duration of the battle through nature's signs, and even if the seer had been present, Thucydides shows us in his history how ironically unreliable such interpretations could be. Despite the skepticism his observance of intractable human nature bred in him, he miscalculates badly the time it would take for this particular folly to play out.

Though Thucydides' chronicle is broken up into years and seasons, this long expanse of historical time, unlike novels set in and controlled by historical periods with narrative neatness, has the same unmarked duration and repetitive patterns as epic time, with no clear beginning or end. Horace remarks favorably on the way Homer starts *The Iliad* in medias res, for had he chosen the whole war with a certain beginning and ending, it would have been too much for our comprehension.[6] In fact, it would have made no difference, for within this timeless time, participants are continually replaced by others who repeat the patterns of fighting and of dying. Events, though they have their climaxes, turn first to one side, then another, and that is as much variety or progress as we are likely to find in the epic. We might say the same of Thucydides' incomplete history.

By contrast, no matter where the story begins or ends in the traditional novel, the beginning and the end are significant points in a chosen segment of life – in the picaresque, a resolution, in the Bildungsroman, an illumination, though we may come into the novel before the starting point through memory, and move into the future through resignation, hope or fear.

Heraclitus presents war as the prime example of the world's constant flux and instability, but in fact, it is war that is the one unchanging entity, whose patterns hold, despite all varieties, in Homer and Thucydides. When Nietzsche declares that practically every era of Western civilization has at one time or another tried to liberate itself from the Greeks,[7] it is clear he has a larger meaning in mind, but I choose to take it to signify in particular our attempts to tell a different story, to liberate ourselves from the epic trap.

La Ronde

The uncommon moment of transcendence Akhilleus experiences in his anger when he realizes that "all the rumoured / wealth of Ilium" is not worth one human life,[1] is reflected in Pericles's counsel that "We must cry not over the loss of houses and land but of men's lives; since houses and land do not gain men, but men them."[2] Still, the *basso ostinato* of history is always beating. The universally noted connectives of Thucydides' masterpiece are not and, by, for, yet, conjunctives representing to William James a democratic and social grammar, (and, we might add, a novelistic grammar as well), promising a conversation among equals[3] but rape, plunder, enslavement, slaughter; it is the sheer casualness of it all that is so appalling.

There are few moments in Homer's epic battles when the participants stop to ask what they are doing and why, though there are some who believe the poet himself, unlike his characters, questions motives and morality. Hektor slaughters Skhedios and Aiáx slaughters Laódamas and Poulydamas kills the Kyllânian etc. Virgil gives no ground to Homer as he asks the Muses to "Help me to spread the massive page of war," and then proceeds to inform us how so and so killed so and so to the edge of doom.[4]

In the early days of the Peloponnesian War, the great Pericles, no cupcake he, sails around the Peloponnesus laying waste the sea-coast, driving many behind their walls because of the terror of his appearance.[5] He and his army take part in ravaging Megara, and later Epidaurus, after which they "laid waste the territory of Troezen, Halieis and Hermione…and thence sailing to Prasiae…ravaged part of its territory, and took and sacked the place itself; after which they returned home"….[6] A typical fine day's work.

In the second year of the war, the Athenians feel justified in slaughtering the Corinthian Aristeus and his allies whom they had persuaded the Thracians to relinquish. They then throw their bodies into a pit to match the same stratagem the Spartans had begun when "they slew and cast into pits all the Athenian and allied traders whom they caught on board the merchantmen round the Peloponnesus."[7]

But don't go imagining the Thracians, who had delivered Aristeus and his allies, are passive abettors. Thucydides tells us, in fact, they were most bloody when they had nothing to fear. Bursting into Mycalessus, they sacked the houses and temples, butchered the inhabitants whether young or old, women or animals. Nothing, according to the historian, during the whole war came near, "in suddenness and horror",[8] to their massacre of all the children of a boys' school in the nineteenth year of the conflict.

After a spirited debate, in the fifth year of the war, concerning the fate of the Mytileneans on the island of Lesbos who were considering defection from the Athenian empire, the Athenians decided against Cleon's draconian punishment but nevertheless proceeded, in what Thucydides called a "savage" action, to kill one thousand ringleaders, to ethnically cleanse the island and redistribute the land to Athenian settlers, "essentially wip[ing] out the aristocracy of Lesbos in one fell swoop."[9]

In the seventh year of the war, the Messanians fled when more than a thousand of them had been killed by the Naxians, but that surely didn't stop them, in their turn, from falling upon, routing and killing. Seeing this, the Athenians landed from their ships and fell upon the disordered Messanians, pushing them into the city, setting up a trophy, and sailing to Rhegium. After this, the Hellenes in Sicily continued to make war on each other by land without the Athenians.[10]

In the twentieth year of the war, the Spartans, following their admiral, were blown off course to some islands. Since they were stuck there for eight days, what better occupation than to plunder and consume all the Clazomenian property. Nor were they willing to let nature have the last word as chief destroyer. The admiral Asyochus, landing at the Meropid Cos, sacked the city, which had lately been laid in ruins by an earthquake.[11]

But pillage was simply the weak sister of slaughter. In *The Iliad*, the generally wise Nestor hurries his men onto the more important of two activities: "...no one should linger over booty now. / ...Now is the time to kill them! Later on / strip them at leisure when they lie here dead!"[12] When Meneláos feels the urge to succumb to pity, he is checked by his brother Agamémnon. "Once in our hands not one should squirm away from death's hard fall! No fugitive, not even / the manchild carried in a woman's belly...."[13] One is tempted to think, with the keeper of the horde in *Beowulf*, that "pillage and slaughter / have emptied the earth of entire peoples."[14]

The best and most famous exchange in the whole of Thucydides takes place between the Athenians, who, in the sixteenth year of war, are attempting to persuade the Melians to be ruled by Athens, and the Melians, who wish to remain neutral. Here the Athenians proclaim the oft-quoted melancholy conditions of human history: "...you know as well as we do that right, as the world goes, is only in question between equals in power, while the strong do what they can and the weak suffer what they must."¹⁵ The Melians refuse the Athenian request to submit and have later to surrender. The grown men are put to death, the women and children sold for slaves, while the Athenians send out five hundred colonists and settle the place themselves.¹⁶

But, like Zeus' scale, history's seems to move up or down with arbitrariness. The stronger become the weaker, the vanquished become vanquishers, pursuers are pursued. The attacked Athenian ships counter-attack and pursue the pursuing Peloponnesians, who flee in turn. The Athenians capture six of their ships and repossess their own vessels which had been lost earlier. A Corinthian company routs the Athenians and pushes them to the sea, but the Athenians and Carystians, in their turn, drive the Corinthians from the ships.¹⁷ When, in *The Iliad*, Arês wants revenge after his son dies in the fighting, Athêna reminds him (one wouldn't imagine the god of war would need such reminding) that "By now / some better man than he in strength and skill has met his death in battle, or soon will. / There is no saving all the sons of mankind."¹⁸

Yet the need for vengeance cannot be sated. The Athenian heroes, those who died for their country, says Pericles, held "that vengeance upon their enemies was more to be desired than any personal blessings."¹⁹ And vengeance drives the epic plot in which the vanquished becomes the vanquisher. As he expires, Homer's Orodës whispers: "whoever you are, you'll not take joy / In his death long, for it will be avenged. An equal destiny awaits you here. / The same field will be yours to lie in soon."²⁰ Of course, in the long run, this pattern gets you nowhere, but there is a kind of lazy security in the repetition of scene, in the comfortable unquestioning acceptance of fate so characteristic of the Homeric epic, which takes place in a world at one with those who live and die in it.

Looking ahead to a partially Christian *Beowulf*, it is still "always better / to avenge dear ones than to indulge in mourning. / For every one of us, living in this world / means waiting for our end. Let whoever can / win glory before death. When a warrior is gone, / that will be his best and only bulwark.²¹

Only the novel, which has separated itself from the epic formulas, can do parodic justice to this model. In Italo Calvino's marvelous satiric spoof, "The Nonexistent Knight", an officer in the pavilion of the Superintendency of Duels, Feuds and Besmirched Honor concludes that the best way for Raimbaut to avenge his father, a general, is to kill three majors or four captains. And another calculates that we count an uncle's vendetta as half a father's.[22]

After so many years of fighting in Thucydides' narrative, victory and defeat mean nothing. In the eighteenth year, after an unsuccessful attack upon a Syracusan fort, the Athenians move on with the fleet and army to the river Terias, then march inland, laying waste the plain and burning the grain, killing some of the Syracusan party and then, of course, setting up the conventional trophy, before returning to their ships. The following year, a naval battle off Erineus has taken place, after which both sides erect trophies of victory, though the Corinthians are grateful simply for having avoided defeat and the Athenians ambivalent for not having won decisively.[23]

Smelling blood as the Athenians foolishly attack, the Syracusans were so eager to fight they simply went back to the docks where the market had been relocated so they could grab a quick sandwich and still make the show on time, a far cry from the Homeric great globs of meat washed down with wine, "shambling cattle butchered, and fat sheep; young porkers by the litter, crisp with fat / ... singed and spitted in Hephaistos' fire," all the savory flesh one craved,[24] without the burden of post-prandial flossing. In a later *Ulysses*, Bloom is disgusted by the way peace and war depend on some "fellow's digestion... Slaughter of innocents. Eat drink and be merry. Then casual wards full after. Heads bandaged."[25]

As the Athenian aggression is countered effectively, things go from bad to worse. The Athenian troops march, under siege, to the Assinarus river, driven by thirst and hoping for safety. But when they see the Syracusans waiting for them, they lose any discipline they have left and rush to drink even the foul water in which they are being butchered. Nicias surrenders to Gylippus and they start on a march during which more men will die than in any other action of the Sicilian battles. Those Athenians and their allies taken prisoners are held in quarries, suffering now, in turn what they must at the hands of those who are doing what they can. The leaders of the captured are executed, the quarry workers sold as slaves after eight months of hard labor and many deaths.[26]

The Athenians fall off the merry-go-round with the disaster of final defeat in the Ionian wars, within the Peloponnesian struggle, at the hands of the Spartan Admiral Lysander at Aegospotami. With short periods of oligarchy, their democracy, the intellectual and commercial center of Greece, remains vital until the Macedonian conquest.[27] Sparta goes on until 394 when it gets its comeuppance at the hands of Persia just ten years after the defeat of Athens. (The shrewd Persian Tissaphernes saw how he could use the worn plot by playing one side against the other[28] until, like the gingham dog and the calico cat, his enemies might eat each other up.)

The wheel has come full circle from the Persian Wars. But as the nature of wheels is to roll on, Alexander the Great steps onto the stage from Macedonia to conquer in 334 and rule over Greece and Persia. The way is clear when, in 331, the last great king, Darius the Third, dies in flight, but death finds Alexander ten years later in Babylon.

And Death Shall Have no Distinction

Though they fight for individual glory, there are no personal novelistic distinctions to be made, no deep interior life, between two masses meeting on the field among "rivulets of blood",[1] groans and shouts of triumph alternating from those who kill and those who are killed. "Out of doors," Oscar Wilde observes, "one becomes abstract and impersonal. One's individuality absolutely leaves one,"[2] so it is only reasonable to liken men, as Homer and Virgil do, to inert nature and natural phenomena, conflagrations, floods, fields of wheat under a scythe. And this intertwining comes easily because nature is adequate,[3] and not alienating, as it was to be in later centuries.

It stands to reason that in Homer and Thucydides, the two sides often cannot tell one another apart, underscoring the irrationality of the whole testosteronic endeavor. The Acarnanians began to pursue the Peloponnesians, but they killed only the Ambraciots, "there being much dispute and difficulty in distinguishing whether a man was an

Ambraciot or a Peloponnesian."[4] In the battle of Sybota early in the war, the number of the triremes on both sides, Corinth and Corcyra, (these two central to the beginning of the whole mess), made it difficult, once they mixed it up, to distinguish between the conquering and the conquered.[5] Retreating in the darkness, soldiers killed one another, mistaking them for the enemy.

In the hoplite battles, vision was so limited by helmets and their small eye slots, by dust and crowded fields, "mistaken identity was commonplace, given, as well, that distinctive uniforms and national insignia were often absent."[6] It is not surprising that during the war, in all conformations – hoplite, triremes, cavalry, blockade, siege – free men became slaves and slaves free.

At one point in the conflict between the Syracusans and the Athenians, the soldiers could not tell who was who even in bright moonlight, distinguishing only the forms of the body, but not whether they were friend or foe. The singing of war paeans while marching into battle[7] confused matters more since the two sides used similar chants. In any case, when a democracy attacks a democracy, the distinctions of war make little sense.

Agamémnon tells his brother to "let [their enemy] all without distinction perish, / every last man of Ilion, / without a tear, without a trace!"[8] The only distinction we can find on the battlefield is the manner in which they die. Though many have complained about the sameness of slaughter in the epics, as a kind of "narrative stupidity,"[9] one of the best translators of *The Iliad* and *The Odyssey*, with little irony, points out that Homer is wonderfully inventive in varying his lurid effects,[10] which become more formulaic in the long line of his imitators.

Time after time a man falls and armor clangs upon him, but he and the man next to him have been killed in different ways. There is a slashing of the belly near the navel allowing all the bowels to drop out uncoiling on the ground, there is the arrow punching through the right buttock, past the pelvic bone, into the bladder, lengthening the victim like an earthworm as dark blood flows and stains the ground, there is a forehead hit with a jagged stone, the frontal bone giving way, both eyes bursting from their sockets, dropping into the dust before Patróklos' feet, there is my personal favorite, the spearhead splitting the white brain pan, teeth dashed out, blood filling both eyes and spurting from mouth and nostrils, there is the helmeted head severed from a tender neck and set in the dust, the spear still in the eye-socket, the head lifted like a poppy and the trunk in another place on the field, the remaining torsos, of course, being particularly without distinction."[11]

And if differences are to come about only through a variety of hacking, Virgil must be doubly imaginative, for he has twins to deal with. Pallas makes a "grim distinction: Now Evander's blade / Cut Thymber's head off while for you, Laridës, / Dying fingers of your right hand, severed,/ Fluttered as they groped for the sword hilt."[12]

When might holds sway, says Simone Weil, "it makes a thing of man in the most literal sense, for it makes him a corpse."[13] And if the realm of might makes a corpse of man, it makes an object of woman. In *The Iliad*, when the dead are piled on a wagon, the women are separated from their children and sold as slaves, (as were both the children and the women in the Peloponnesian War), or the women were taken in as mistresses by their enemies. While the winner at the canonical epic funeral games in the Greek camp receives a tripod worth 12 oxen, the loser is rewarded with a woman skilled in crafts and valued at 4 oxen.[14]

With difficulty but with no self-consciousness, the two factions figured out which corpse belonged to which side, piling them on their pyre, the fire a great equalizer. When Homer's groups "met on the battlefield" they had difficulty "distinguishing the dead men, one by one. ...sick at heart therefore / in silence they piled corpses on the pyre / and burned it down. Then back they went to Iilion. / Just so on their side the Akhaians piled / dead bodies on their pyre, sick at heart, / and burned it down. Then back to the ships they went."[15]

The Trojans and the Akhaians, and later, the Latins heaped up the carnage, "bodies jumbled, / Numberless and nameless."[16] Despite the novelistic feeling for the individual in Ian McEwan's *Atonement*, the First World War causes the narrator to remark "How quickly the dead faded into each other, so that Sergeant Mooney's face became Private Lowell's, and both exchanged their fatal wounds with those of other men whose names they could no longer recall."[17]

There is this though. The ancient heroes with distinguished names could sometimes bring distinction to those they slaughtered. Thus the shade of Lausus, since the Parcae insisted upon his early death, has the consolation, at least, of having died "by the sword-thrust of great Aeneas."[18] At a later time, Don Quixote would curse artillery as "a device by means of which an infamous and cowardly arm may take the life of a valiant knight, without his knowing how or from where the blow fell...a random bullet, fired, it may be, by someone who fled in terror...,"[19] and our mass murder machines have only become in their terrible efficiency all the more impersonal.

The Myth of Progress

The epic mode in Homer and Thucydides unfurls back and forth down a one-dimensional plane. In his great funeral oration, Pericles makes the obligatory nod to those, outnumbered two to one, who fought the battle of Marathon with Miltiades, and to our fathers who enlarged this empire we now possess.[1] ("Delium was the first battle in or on the border of Attica since Marathon," Victor Davis Hanson observes, "and it would prove as embarrassing as that earlier victory...had been glorious.")[2] Later, the general Hippocrates too will look back in order to look forward, drawing inspiration for his troops from those who fought at Oenophyta with Myronides. The Athenians are quick to tell the Spartans that they acquired their empire through the Delian League not by force but because they were the saviors of the Hellenic world, fighting alone before help arrived.[3] And if our ancestors, Pericles continues, with fewer resources than ours, successfully overcame the Persians, all the more must we not fall behind but combat our enemies in such a way that we can "hand down our power to our posterity unimpaired."[4]

Coming after Homer and Pericles, Virgil wants to move tendentiously towards a golden age, while questioning the price of empire building, but he is also obliged to pay homage, like his predecessors, to past glories. The shield that Vulcan makes for Aeneas depicts elaborately both past and future. When Aeneas sees the Trojan battles represented on the wall of a Carthaginian temple, he is moved to wonder "What spot on earth…is not full of the story of our sorrow?'"[5] Virgil's Dido has a history of her own engraved on the gold and silver plates used to honor her guests, showing "brave deeds of her fathers, / A sequence carried down through many captains/ In a long line from the founding of the race."[6]

The story of Troy carries on through the ages and is especially welcome as epic history by Don Quixote, who equates the site of his defeat by the Knight of the White Moon to Troy, and finds the stories on the wall tapestries of a hostelry challenging, for had he been born in that age, "Troy would not have been burned nor Carthage destroyed…."[7] But of course, the knight and his squire have to move forward because, after all, they are creating another "epic". Sancho wagers that there will be no alehouse, inn, tavern, barbershop where the history of their exploits will not be painted on the wall.

The epic narrative commands its heroes to leave, in the words of Pericles, "more history in their wake to inspire a new generation for battle."[8] The young men of Athens whose fathers had been killed fighting for their country are educated at public expense and paraded around the theatre where they are presented with a set of armor, which starts up a new mindless epic of repetition.

Squeezed between Homer and Virgil, the Athenians are caught up in a cycle that simply follows the predictable recapitulation in which fathers and sons keep the pot boiling. Hektor projects what followers will say of his own son, like him a Trojan prince, that "'this fellow is far better than his father!' / seeing him home from war, and his arms / the bloodstained gear of some tall warrior slain –/ making his mother proud."[9]

Aeneas tells his son Ascanius to take as his models his Uncle Hektor (we remember Andrómakhê explaining to her son that his father "was no moderate man in war…/ And that is why they mourn him through the city,")[10] and his own father, who introduced him to "the boons of war."[11] Telémakhos learns skill and craftiness from his father, Odysseus, whose fame as a fighting man "has echoed in my ears."[12]

There is, in fact, no moving off into by-paths and indirections promising new life – possibilities which are always present in the novel – only a timeless swinging back and forth. Akhilleus seems to be a tragic hero by making a choice to give up a life of common routine in favor of a briefer but more glorious life and death, but in point of fact, his life, despite a greater spectrum of mood and a higher fierceness of fighting, is a life of epic routine after all. The gods know his story which his mother has told him. These heroes will never have that novelistic choice that Henry James speaks of when he exploits his moral subtleties playing out on a multi-dimensional plane. The epic story belongs to the will of the gods.

There is, in fact, a grimly narrowed choice in the epic mode but it doesn't amount to very much. No use telling us, as Pericles does in the last speech to come down to us, that for those who have a free choice in the matter and whose fortunes are not at stake, "war is the greatest of follies," because the epic wars of literature and history are always presented to the young as a "choice…between submission with loss of independence, and danger with the hope of preserving that independence"; in such cases, "it is he who will not accept the risk that deserves blame, not he who will."[13]

Reading the Heroic Story Poorly

Pericles boasts that Athens does not need a Homer or any other poet whose verses "melt at the touch of fact."[1] But he himself is writing both history and a Homeric epic, featuring Athenians who fight with the ferocity and frequency of the Achaians. Though Hector, and reluctantly, Akhilleus, fought for their great states, and for vengeance, it was personal glory which ranked highest in their minds. Not so the Athenians, whose polis was their guiding star. (Even Sparta, though hardly a democracy, moved from a more primitive ethic to one of citizenship, whose virtues are displayed within the hoplite phalanx ranks ready to die for their state.)[2]

By marking Athens as standing for a more than adequate destiny, Pericles gives his citizens the inner security of the epic hero.[3] In his funeral oration, he is faced with a difficult task, for if he praises the fallen comrade of a friend in the audience and leaves out some of what should have been included, he will be accused of not telling the truth, and if he is too fulsome in his praise, he will raise envy in the listener who will "suspect exaggeration if he hears anything above his own nature."⁴ The thing to do, then, is to follow the epic pattern but give the city and community pride of place, and this he proceeds to accomplish.

He lauds Athens as he does its fallen soldiers, appreciates its festivals, the elegance of its private establishments, the rich produce which enters its harbor from the whole world, the artistic treasures, providing the citizens with daily inspiration and distracting them from distress, athletic and dramatic competitions the year round, exemplary moral equivalents of war. No accident, then, that it is in war Homer's Nestor recalls his games: "Would god / I had my young days back, my strength entire... That day, no one / gave me a match...."⁵ I was victorious, he boasts, in boxing, in wrestling, in the quarter mile, in the javelin-throw.⁶ Heroism, writes Ortega, is a "sublime 'sporting' attitude" through which life shows "a vital grace which can never grow old."⁷

Pericles turns Nietzsche's clever insight that every principle is a forgotten metaphor on its head. "Unrivaled by any other in resources of magnitude," the city inspires heroic deeds, artistic achievements and a high quality of life for citizens yet unknown. When they look upon the Acropolis, they are filled with love and pride, as Pericles knew they would be. You, citizens "must yourselves realize the power of Athens, and feed your eyes upon her from day to day, till love of her fills your hearts."⁸

Taking advantage of a period of peace between 446 and 432 B.C., Pericles has the Parthenon and the Propylaea constructed. The city on the hill challenged Olympus. Though the exterior colonnade of the Parthenon presented the traditional subjects of mythic gods and heroes, the decorative frieze around the Parthenon's internal chamber represented humans for the first time in Greek history. It was men who had defeated the Persians, not gods.

At that time Athens was becoming the cultural center of the Greek world, with plays of the great tragedians staged, with philosophers and scientists attracted to the intellectual ferment. Before he died in the second year of the war, Pericles could truly boast that the city on the hill was "greater than any hitherto known, the memory of which will descend to the latest posterity."⁹ He recognizes, in a broader sense, the "general law of decay", but even if such a fate should happen to Athens, its glory will remain eternal in history. Pericles never ceases to strut his stuff. Whatever happens, we will always be able to say that "We ruled the largest group of Hellenic states and sustained the greatest wars..., achievements which may engender a desire for emulation in more generous breasts, and a feeling of hatred and envy for those who cannot match us."[10]

Of course, not everyone believed in Pericles' story. Despite "the cultivation of refinement without extravagance and knowledge without effeminacy and wealth more for use than for show,"[11] the lavish spending required for such a city (nothing compared to what the war would cost) caused resentment, and the religious elements of society found that the extensive adornment made Athens look like "a wanton woman."[12] OK, then, says Pericles, let the costs go to my account and the inscriptions on the buildings stand in my name. Well, no one wants to be left out of a great story so they opened up the public purse. (There is no lesson here for Congress since art gives little glory in this country).

We will never know how much of his story Pericles believed himself, for a politician as canny as he knew that he was balancing the hopes and the fears of his audience, "with one to check undue confidence and the other to raise and cheer them."[13] But if we are to accept Nietzsche's measurement of the strength of a spirit as how much of the truth one would be able to stand,[14] Homer's warriors, and by extension, the Athenians, would, in some respects, score well. Clear eyed and fearless, they answer the death they know is coming in the name of Troy and all Akhaia while giving death to others. And in Pericles' oration of 431, the heroes who die for Athens are without regrets. The measure of Athens' greatness is taken in the expenditure of "more lives and effort in warfare than any other polis."[15]

In another respect, however, Pericles sugar-coats the heroic narrative. In praising the fallen at Samos, he likens those who die for their country to the immortal gods, to whom we pay honors though we do not see them, but whom we know by their benefits.[16] Athens knows her sons by their benefits as well, and does not see them. Those left behind are blinded by the "story", in which the fallen will be eternally remembered upon "every occasion on which deed or story shall be commemorated,"[17] not unlike the deeds and heroes of Homer.

As personages in an epic story, the Athenians cannot escape the limitations of their imagination, those limitations the Syracusan Hermocrates recognizes as well in addressing the Sicilians. Everyone knows war is an evil, that peace would be desirable if both sides should happen to have chosen the wrong moment for belligerency, "and this, if we did but see it is just what we stand most in need of at the present juncture."[18] If we did but see it! (In the novel, the character who does not read well, and those who love her, suffer the consequences, as illustrated so dramatically by James' Isabel Archer. But reading poorly in an epic is likely to have consequences considerably more extensive.)

In his funeral oration, Pericles claims that Athenians are unique in uniting daring and deliberation at their highest point. They looked upon "discussion" not as a "stumbling block in the way of action...but [as] an indispensable preliminary to any wise action at all."[19] In fact, his countrymen turn out to be not only poor readers but poor listeners, as well, who feel it unnecessary, given their own glorious story, to heed those of others, generally attentive to men of bad advice and dismissive of men with sage counsel. (Long after his death, Pericles' countrymen approve of Alcibiades' argument for engagement in Sicily rather than Nicias' wiser counsel; echoing in our ears is the troop's roar of approval for Hektor's poor tactics, "Pallas Athêna having taken away their wits.")[20]

An age in which religion is fading but omens are still heeded invites poor reading. When the plague strikes, this inadequacy of the Athenians becomes almost laughably serviceable. The people remembered an old prophecy about a coming pestilence, but they argue over whether dearth or death had been the key word, and seeing death all around, they choose that.[21] Even the more sober of the Athenians allowed omens to affect their judgment. In the nineteenth year of the war, the Athenians want to leave Syracuse in a big way, though their reluctant leader Nicias would have preferred an honorable death in the field to a dishonorable execution in Athens, only to have an eclipse of the moon – Nicias was "somewhat overaddicted to divination and practices of that kind" – change their minds, persuading them to wait at least 27 days, as prescribed by soothsayers.[22] Things go from bad to worse, and Nicias must have felt, like Hecuba, that the gods were wretched things to call on for help,[23] but after a decisive naval defeat, he hoped the enemy would be inclined to look upon the soldiers more kindly as objects of pity rather than jealousy.[24] Alas, no pity is shown them. Following the advice given by devious messengers to put off their leaving, they fall into an ambush, whereupon the Athenians suffer catastrophic losses.

Long after Pericles disappears from the narrative, in the fifth year of the war, Thucydides talks about the characteristics of revolution, which, beyond the lack of moderation, feature "the ability to see all sides of a question" and the "incapacity to act on any…."[25] Unfortunately, this was never the Athenians' problem. Besotted with their gloriously heroic history, more than a twice-told tale, the Athenians hope for the kind of smug peace Hardy tells us in "The Dynasts" poor reading represents.

Woefully deficient, as well, was their reading of the stories others carried. The Corinthians argue, in the early days, that the Athenians ought to pay attention to past favors and not incur their enmity to secure a naval alliance, since "kindness opportunely shown has a greater power of removing old grievances than the facts of the case may warrant."[26] (Lysistrata makes the same argument to the Athenian and Spartan negotiators – "So why on fighting are your hearts so set? / For each of you is in the other's debt. / Why don't you make peace? What's the problem?")[27] But the argument holds little sway with them because neither the appreciation of nor the interest in the harvest of sown resentment stirs them in the least. Athenians should be willing to go to war whether the cause be great or small, and that's that.[28]

Of course, Pericles is aware they will be sowing hatred among the vanquished which will be, however, short-lived. What makes "the splendor of the present and the glory of the future remains forever unforgotten."[29] But he does not have to be sensitive to the morals of his story; indeed, we question whether, in his time and place, he has the moral imagination (the essence of the nineteenth-century novel) to be so, for "everywhere, whether for evil or for good, we have left imperishable monuments behind us."[30] There is not a hint of remorse.

Pericles tells his people they hold "a tyranny; to take it perhaps was wrong, but to let it go is unsafe."[31]

And no holds barred. The great Spartan leader Brasidas considered it more disgraceful for "persons of character"[32] to take what they want by fraud than by open force, but the Athenians have no such qualms. Pericles accepts deceit as a necessary weapon of arms though he tells the Athenians it is only the love of honor, not of gain, that never grows old.[33] And long into the war, his countrymen show no reluctance in ruthlessly slaughtering those to whom they promise safety. What the Athenians fail to appreciate is that deception is most easily practiced on those who cannot read well, and they themselves will fall victim to a fatal ambush at the end of the war.

One thing can be said for deception, however. Unpalatable as such double-dealings might be, they promise more twists and turns than the tit for tat slaughter on the battlefield. Odysseus, the great trickster[34] and tactician (remember Hektor's "poor tactics") is never boring, and no wonder – Athêna calls this "contriver," of all men living, "the best in plots and story telling."[35] (In *The Aeneid*, where the Trojan horse ploy is described most vividly, he is transformed into the arch villain of lies, slipperiness, brutal treachery.)[36] This is one epic hero who could waltz into the novel – "God help us all," Don Quixote says, "this world is nothing but schemes and plots, all working at cross purposes."[37] There's a bit of Tom Sawyer in Odysseus as well.

To his credit, Pericles, the historian tells us, advises a strategy of waiting quietly, maintaining the naval force, attempting no new conquests, and avoiding hazards to the city,[38] but the Athenians do the very opposite. In any case, Athens' sanctions against the Megarians in 432 – the Megarian Decree, hardly covered by Thucydides – and Pericles' inflexibility in the matter as he insisted upon strict adherence to every detail, are generally considered, along with the Corinthian intervention in Epidamnus which brought the Corcyreans into the conflict, prime instigators of the war.[39]

In "The Acharnians", Aristophanes' Dikaiopolis doesn't think it's fair to blame it all on Sparta and their incursions into Attica. No, war broke out early "because Pericles, Olympian Pericles…began making laws written like drinking songs, "No Megarian shall stand / On sea or on land, / And from all of our markets they're utterly banned." He complains that "First it was their woolies, before long, whenever they saw anyone with a watermelon, or a young hare or a piglet, or some garlic and rock-salt, 'Ah!' they said, 'Megarian contraband', and had them confiscated...."[40]

Dikaiopolis points a finger at the Athenian citizens, then at the aliens among them, but it was not the city, mind you. Aristophanes is playing with the assignment of blame but his sarcasm pays tribute, in a negative sort of way, to the power of Pericles' extravagant epic romance of Athens, its enlightened government and its heroic citizens. "Unlike any other nation" or "alone of her contemporaries" or "a pattern to others"[41] are phrases that understandably come easily to Pericles. Thucydides promised an absence of romance[42] but his protagonist presents plenty of it. Our constitution and laws are not derived from others but are copied by them.[43] Tested, Athens always turns out to be even greater than reputed.[44] When the Spartans invade our country, they have to bring with them all their confederates, but Athenians advance into another's territory without help, and usually "vanquish with ease men who are defending their homes."[45]

Of course this Athenian romance was readily believed because it fed upon the national temperament, which, once got going, was difficult to control. "Born into the world to take no rest themselves" as the Corinthians describe the Athenians, they "give none to others."[46] It is no small irony that these Greeks turn out to most resemble Homer's Trojans, who "will not get their fill of fighting."[47] Alcibiades, far into the seventeenth summer of the war, cleverly plays into this temperament. Once he assures his audience that "the safest rule of life is to take one's character and institutions for better and for worse, and to live up to them as closely as one can," he is able to argue persuasively that "a city inactive by nature couldn't choose a quicker way to ruin itself than by suddenly adopting a policy of peace...."[48]

So strong is his belief in the romance he weaves, that Pericles imagines it would be almost a pleasure to be vanquished by such an illustrious opponent as Athens and should bring no blush to the face of the defeated.[49] For a civilization without equal, a natural attitude would be one of condescension towards those less endowed, and indeed, this becomes a key Athenian characteristic. In the second year of the war, Pericles argues that his countrymen must confront their enemies "not merely with spirit but with disdain...which is the privilege of those who, like us, have been assured by reflection of their superiority to their adversary."[50] And how quickly, in the siege of Pylos, once the troops see a weakness in the Spartan force, "their fear chang[es] to disdain."[51] Yet it has often been said that the attitudes most frowned upon by the Greeks were pride, arrogance, insolence and self-indulgence![52]

By contrast, fierce Brasidas, "not being a bad speaker for a Spartan,"[53] persuades others through his moderation, fairness and absence of deceit. Furthermore, the women and children of cities he captures are treated with decency and respect. He could induce others to revolt through his "just and moderate conduct,"[54] which certainly left more good will in its wake than Athenian behavior.

Though the Spartans were no strangers to treachery, the Athenians have the nerve to call them the most conspicuous of men in "considering what is agreeable honorable, and what is expedient just,"[55] while advising the Melians that it would be good for them to serve and allow the Athenians to rule because by submitting they would avoid suffering the worst, and the Athenians should gain by not destroying them.[56]

But such arrogance can cause the Athenians to be led astray, which prompts Phormio, in the third year of the war, to argue that precisely because his Athenian men were outnumbered, they should enter a battle, for "the Peloponnesians fear our irrational audacity more than they would ever have done a more commensurate preparation."[57] Subsequently, the Peloponnesians lure him into the straits and capture nine of his triremes.

And finally, such an outsized pride could end up being a powerful tool in the hands of the Syracusan leader Gylippus when he tells his troops that once men are checked in what they consider their special excellence, their whole opinion of themselves suffers more than if they had not at first believed in their superiority.[58] Since the Athenians would accept nothing but total victory, they were routed.

Thucydides reminds us that "it is a habit of mankind to entrust to careless hope what they long for, and to use sovereign reason to thrust aside what they do not desire."[59] Thus the Athenians, who warned the Melians that hope is fine for those who have "abundant resources," but tends towards extravagance, so that one can easily be ruined by staking everything under its enchantment,[60] were unable to recognize their own extravagance as part of a story, and incapable of reading others. They met the fate they had predicted for the Melians.

It would be natural to assume that the Spartans, who brought up their young in barracks, which they seldom left, even after marriage, and who learned the martial arts from the cradle would take easily to war, and though it could be said technically that Sparta had more responsibility for starting the war in 431 (some thought Corinth was to blame when they fought Corcyra at sea or when Plataea was attacked by Thebans), but compared with the Athenians, and despite their nasty habit of throwing prisoners live into a pit "where the disabled and wounded slowly starved or bled to death,"[61] not to mention their harsh treatment of their helots, they were more reluctant to fight or break peace treaties than their classic enemy. In truth, if the Spartans were not more peace-loving, they were certainly more cautious. Though they habitually saw Athens as a threat to the Hellenic world, they were slow to enter any war and eager for peace whenever possible.

In earlier days, the Spartan king, Archidamus, expressed great wariness[62] about any kind of belligerent engagement with the Athenians. His countrymen's temperament tended to be conservative and their belief in omens and sacrifices provided another brake on rash behavior. Before the war began, they had already recognized that the Athenians had breached the treaty, but they inquired of the god at Delphi whether or not they should engage them. Well, if you put your whole strength into the conflict, was the answer, victory will be yours.[63] Not exactly incorrect, either.

In the seventh year of the war, the Spartan envoys try to persuade the Athenians to cooperate in drawing up a peace treaty that would bring Attica and Sparta into accord, allowing them both to rule the Hellenic world while avoiding the creation of vengeful enemies, but the disdainful Athenians, swayed by Cleon, reject the offer, a rejection which Thucydides reads as an ill-advised attempt "to grasp for something more."[64] (This pattern was repeated again even after the Sicilian disaster when they refused an offer of peace from Sparta, playing defense between 410 and 407,[65] before they lived to regret it). Indeed, as time passes, the Athenians begin to wonder about the wisdom of their refusal. Growing weary of the siege of Pylos which was taking longer than they had anticipated, they brought it to an end under Cleon, while plundering from the Spartans and sowing the seeds of resentment which would come back to haunt them.[66] (When, in the sixteenth year of the war, Sparta refrained from breaking off the treaty, they nevertheless proclaimed that any of their people might plunder the Athenians.)[67]

By the tenth year, feeling more vulnerable than once they had, the Athenians again regret their rejection of the peace opportunity at Pylos. But again luck is with them, for the Spartans, plagued by the Helots' revolt, feel a need for a respite. The two sides draw up the treaty of Nicias that is supposed to last fifty years, as unreasonable a number as one could find. The peace lasted almost seven years but was unstable, fractured by continual incursions and hostilities. And no wonder, with the "in your face" attitude of the Athenians, who, on a commemorative pillar set up in the Acropolis, inscribed the words: "The Spartans have not abided by their oaths, just three years after the signing,"[68] thereby thumbing the collective Athenian nose at it, and ravaging Laconia in 414.

A second diner in "Lysistrata" suggests that the Athenians should be drunk when going on diplomatic missions for "we couldn't be as stupid as we are when we're sober.... As it is, you see, we go to Sparta sober, and so we're always looking for catches. We can't hear what they do say, and we hunt for implications in what they don't say...."[69] In any case, such a treaty, far from making a new beginning, simply facilitates the turning over and over of the same tired plot. Each group gives up territory it had conquered.[70] Yet the fecklessness of the entire adventure does not seem to have occurred to them. With no desire to read the other's story, they were left "ignorant of the territory's size and of the number of its inhabitants...."[71] Athens falls under the spell of Alcibiades' story and takes on the fatal Sicilian invasion.

Still, even after Athens was on the ropes, suffering huge losses in Sicily towards the end of the war, the Spartans, who had the opportunity to besiege the Piraeus, "proved the most convenient people in the world for Athenians to be at war with."[72] By delaying their actions, they gave Athens time to build a new navy. "The wide difference between the two characters, the slowness and want of energy of the Spartans as contrasted with dash and enterprise of opponents, proved of the greatest service, especially to a maritime empire like Athens." Finally, however, conditions become so painful and irreparable for Athens the luxury of a lazy regret could no longer be indulged. Peace came on much less favorable terms than she could have won in 425.[73]

The Public Epic

Because we view Thucydides' account as an epical one, we are not surprised that we cannot find a sustained tension of opposing forces between the public and private realms, despite the fact that the author, as we have noted, lived in an age which tended to see things in paired rhetorical opposites[1]: military history favored the Thucydidian preference by neatly dividing the multifaceted war into two large antagonistic forces, Athens and Sparta, the naval and the land powers, democracy and oligarchy, pro and con ambassadorial colloquies.

The dialectic between public and private demands is powerful in the tragedy of "Antigone", and a source of wisdom in the novel but in *The Iliad*, the private agonies of Akhilleus, the angry jealousy of Agamémnon and the death of Patróklos can hardly be balanced against the enormous force they let loose on the field. In the epic mode, the private realm is an afterthought, overwhelmed by the public story. It is at one with history. What, the Lykian Sarpêdôn asks Glaukos, is the point of being honored by prime place at table, choice meats, full cups, and fertile lands granted, unless we fight well in the blaze of battle.[2]

Within the public sphere of activities, riven by continual revolutions in the Peloponnesian War, what private virtues there were become corrupted by public needs. Thucydides tells us that in order to save their democracy, the Corcyreans butchered many of their fellow citizens whom they had come to regard as their enemies. "Death thus raged in every shape...sons were killed by their fathers and suppliants dragged from the altar or slain upon it, while some were even walled up in the temple of Dionysius and died there...."[3] Such behavior Thucydides broadens into a well-known commentary on revolution, in which "reckless audacity came to be considered the courage of a loyal supporter; prudent hesitation, specious cowardice; moderation was held to be a cloak for unmanliness...." The Hellenic "troubles" allowed "every form of iniquity" to take root, and "the ancient simplicity into which honor so largely entered" and which represented so markedly the domestic sphere, "was laughed down and disappeared; and society became divided into camps in which no man trusted his fellow."[4]

Pericles boasts that while the Spartans undergo a "painful discipline"[5] in perfecting the art of manliness, the Athenians can live any way they please and are still prepared for every encounter. Our public men of politics have their private affairs as well, and our simple citizen, occupied as he is with his private life and work, still manages informed judgments about public matters, "for, unlike any other nation, we regard the citizen who takes no part in these duties not as unambitious but as useless."[6] Still, Pericles understood that the Athenians were living in times of imbalance between the two spheres. He asks his fellow citizens, at the outbreak of the plague, to leave their "country" homes and become "rural refugees"[7] by moving to the city for their own safety against disease and invaders, lest the home bleed into the public story, but in fact, the overcrowding simply worsened the plague.

Pericles is clever about hiding from the Athenians the tyranny of the public story in their lives. Whereas previously he had felt free to admit that fighting in the country's battles acts as a cloak which covers private and individual imperfections, (and a good thing, too, for Pericles' private life was rather messy), he now borrows from the public realm to beef up the private one. The offering of the lives of young Athenians in common give them individual renown, their glory not buried in a tomb but eternally remembered in commemorations of deeds and stories, their record written in the heart.[8]

Because those who are left behind suffer the private stories of a nation who celebrates the public glory of dying for one's country, Pericles tries to make the argument that the public sacrifice loved ones have made actually enhances the importance (one might say even the interest) of the private lives. Those are "...fortunate indeed...who draw for their lot a death so glorious as that which has caused your mourning. Still I know that this is a hard saying, especially when you will constantly be reminded by seeing in the homes of others blessings of which once you also enjoyed...." But not to worry. Think of the wonderful stories that will be told and songs sung on every occasion.[9]

Homer's King Alcinous tells the disguised Odysseus there is no need to weep at the song the blind bard Demodocus is singing about him and his fellow Hellenic heroes. After all, the gods "measured the life thread of these men so that their fate might become a poem sung for unborn generations."[10] When Nisus, inspired by the death of his friend Euryalus, avenges him and is killed, Virgil calls both of them Fortunate, because if the poet's songs avail, (and there can be no doubt about that), "no future day will ever take you / Out of the record of remembering Time."[11]

It is the young men left alive who have a bum deal, Pericles tells the mourning mothers, for they must celebrate the deeds of the dead, not be celebrated for the glorious deeds themselves. They have "envy to contend with, while those who are no longer in our path are honored with a goodwill into which rivalry does not enter."[12] Her private life in shambles, Hecuba, in "The Trojan Women", mourns the wretched and wasted death of her grandson when he could have, once grown to manhood, fallen happy in dying for his city.[13] And the heartbroken King Evander cheers himself up wonderfully in *The Aeneid* with the thought that in "manhood's bitter gain / War's hard initiation," his son Pallas drew first blood, and going to an early death took the lives of "countless Volscians" with him.[14] If perchance a soldier might feel some qualms, Pericles has simply to point out that "to a man of spirit, the degradation of cowardice must be immeasurably more grievous than the unfelt death which strikes him in the midst of his strength and patriotism!"[15]

The Iliad is overshadowed by the greatest of public sorrows among men, Simone Weil writes, "the destruction of a city."[16] (Hera is invaluable in that respect. "Whenever my turn comes to lust for demolition of some city / whose people may be favorites of yours," she rages to Zeus, "do not hamper my fury! Free my hands...."[17] And such a sorrow is not lost on the Athenians, for it was the death of a great city, Troy, "rich in gold and rich in bronze,"[18] they had heard about from childhood. Death on the battlefield could provide a few choice passages for the epic but the death of a city engenders more, and it threatens the very heart of the Periclean romance.

Pericles has himself so bought into the importance of his city that when his friends, sitting with him in his final hours, commend his many trophies, he chides them (with a startling lack of empathic imagination) for not making mention of his most impressive achievement, that "no Athenian, through my means, ever wore mourning."[19] Fortunate for him he died early, before the best and brightest of his city perished in the prime of life.

Aristophanes' Lysistrata knows that after men go off to war, there are no more private stories left to tell. She complains "there isn't anyone even to have an affair with – not a sausage!" All we can do, Stratyllis laments, is "cause men to be born" while the public powers "make them die."[20] Then they will return to their mothers, wives and children – "the god of war," writes Aeschylus, "packing smooth the urns with / ashes that once were men."[21]

Only in peace can the private life flourish as the equal of the state's, and to be fair, Pericles had warned the Athenians early on against reckless and ungovernable expansion of empire,[22] but the epic mode demands battle. We could hardly expect a strong private life in a military society like Sparta, (we remember at the beginning of this whole mess Corinth's argument, in supporting Sparta, that the Peloponnesian League should go to war lest it lose the delights of tranquility by remaining inactive.)[23] But the private citizen of Athens foolishly allows himself to be overwhelmed by Alcibiades' arguments that it was a good thing to show the Peloponnesians "how little we care for the peace that we are now enjoying."[24]

On stage it is a different matter. In Aristophanes' comedies, we find the private citizens rebelling against the domination of the public needs, (and in the case of "Lysistrata" overcoming it by the most personal of deprivations). Shortly after Pericles' death, the playwright, in his "Acharnians", has Dikaiopolis take matters into his own hands not for personal glory but for personal peace. "Look, here's eight drachmas," he says to the immortal Amphitheus. "Go to Sparta and make one of those personal peaces you were talking about – for me and the wife and the kids, right?" Not that he expects miracles, of course. A canonical thirty years would do for him.[25]

Even more desperate is a farmer, who begs Dikaiopolis to give him a little bit of the personal peace he possesses, "five years would be enough." And a bridegroom sends his Best Man to beg Dikaiopolis "to give him just a thimbleful of peace, in this bottle. You understand he's keener on making love than war just at the moment."[26]

Trouble brews in the public arena for the same old reason, that men will not listen, especially to the women, traditional keepers of the private hearth. If, argues Lysistrata, wives criticize some blunder the men make, the husband says 'Shut up and mind your own business!' And then they would go out and make an even sillier decision. And if they were criticized again, they would tell their women to go back to their weaving. "Let war be the care of the menfolk."[27]

In a more subtle but equally condescending way, Pericles tells the women, the very keepers of the private life, to keep quiet as well. "If I must say anything on the subject of female excellence to those of you who will now be in widowhood, it be all comprised in this brief exhortation. Great will be your glory in not falling short of your natural character; and greatest will be hers who is least talked of among the men whether for good or for bad."[28] They are not even given the comfort of storytelling, while men will be celebrated publicly in ceremonies and monuments, frieze and song. (Alkinoös asks Odysseus why he should grieve over the Argives and the fall of Troy. "That was all gods' work, weaving ruin there / so it should make a song for men to come!")[29] Though the carrying off of Helen and Briseis represents the origin of the Homeric epic, only as pawns of the state can women be a part of some story, for "...had not the very hand / of God gripped and crushed this city deep in the ground," Euripides' Hecuba moans, " we should have disappeared in darkness, not given / a theme for music, and the songs of men to come."³⁰

While Patróklos lies in state, Akhilleus seems unmoved by the "deep-breasted women / of Troy, and Dardan women," close by who "must lament / and weep hot tears, all those whom we acquired by labor / in assault, by the long spear."³¹ Weeping is the narrative of women who must remain silent guardians of the private story while the public epic will be rehearsed again and again. And the warriors, with this knowledge, generally try to stay clear of domestic contamination. Euryalus in *The Aeneid* has someone else tell his mother he is going into battle.³² Sustaining huge losses, the Trojans might have gone back to Iliam had not Priam's eldest son, Hélenos, argued to Aeneas and Hektor to stand fast before the gates, in effect to remain in the public narrative, lest the men run "pell-mell into the arms of women –/ a great day for our enemies."³³

(In this regard it is sobering to recall it was Sparta who gave, if not the most freedom, the most equality to their women, and it was the Spartan women who were even fiercer than the men, sending their sons to battle with instructions that they should return either with their shields or on them.³⁴ As for baleful Hera-Juno, Queen Woman, her sleepless rage and poisonous mischief are so extreme she needs three epics in which to vent them. "Make the long / ships founder," she orders Aeolus, "Drive them off course! Throw bodies in the sea.")³⁵

It is the power of the public over the private which leads Simone Weil to suggest that the epic, so at home in the world, also expresses, in its quiet way, an earthly homelessness, with only a nostalgic hint of the "far-off world" of peace, family, nature, where the fighting man is everything to those left behind, while those left behind are an "evocation…quickly effaced" on the fields of war.³⁶ Akhilleus' counselors groan for a moment with the remembrance of what each had left at home,³⁷ and Hektor, above all, treasures the secure life of his family and his city, but in an epic, such contrasts between the real and the lyric world are of short duration. (Paris has time to make love to Helen in their fragrant bedroom only because he has been gloriously spirited away from the battlefield by divine intervention).

There will be few furloughs back to the "novelistic" estates, a sense of place, but the epic does allow its warriors to deflect the joys of family onto prideful recitation of personal lineage smack dab in the midst of battle. As Akhilleus throws Asteropaíos into the river, (that river Heraclitus claimed you could never step into twice but which, in the epic mode, belies his assertion) he brags that his parents are even more impressive than his victim's riparian origins, for his begetter, lord over many Myrmidons, was Pêleus, the son of Aiokos, a son of Zeus and his mother Thetis, a daughter of Nereus, man of the sea.[38]

More often, however, the impossibility of returning home is an integral part of battlefield vengeance, enhancing the punishment meted out to the enemy. Pênéleos holds his victim's head up on his sword like a flower and shouts to the Trojans to tell Ilioneus' father and mother to mourn for him. Diomêdês kills Xanthos and Thoôn, the only sons of Phainops, who, worn out by age and misery and empty pain, will never welcome them home again. Later, Diomêdês prefers to let his victims rot "with kites for company, not women," who might mourn and bury them. Aías bursts Lêthos' brains, ending his life "far from Larisa's rich farmland; nor ever would he repay his parents for their care." Akhilleus splits Iphitôn's head in two: "Terror of all soldiers, there you lie! / Here is your place of death! So far away, / your birthplace, near Gygaiê lake, and there / your father's royal parkland on the trout-stream/ Hyllos and the eddying Hermos river!"[39]

If Akhilleus exults in the thought of the fish nibbling away at Lykáôn's white fat, Virgil is not to be outdone by Homer as he has Aeneas roll Tarquitus's headless trunk with his foot, declaring that no gentle mother will bury him but he will be food for the carrion birds or, thrown into the sea, for hungry fishes to nibble his wounds,[40] and so it goes. This is not a dialectical balance but a dialectical sneer, enlarging the glory of the perpetrator on the public battlefield by anticipating the domestic suffering of those left behind.

As weak a force as the domestic scene remains in *The Iliad*, it becomes, nevertheless, a reliable analogue of the repetitive epic and historical plot, the mourning of those left behind and the dying of those who go to war. If, as Tolstoy famously said, all happy families are alike, in the epic, all unhappy families are alike. There is nothing unique in the private sorrows. Iphídamas, a youth of great promise, suffers the fate of many when he leaves "his bridal chamber for the Achaian war" where Agamémnon kills him with a sword thrust across the neck. "Sad that he fought for the townsmen of his bride / and died abroad before he could enjoy her."[41]

And not only brides but beloved wives of longer duration suffer their private story. Andrómakhê mourns the husband who gave his parents grief and pain, and left her "loneliest, and brokenhearted,"[42] weeping for him day and night. Penélopè's story, of course, does stand out in its peculiar characteristics, but, nevertheless, her tears soak her forsaken bed. In *The Aeneid*, "Mothers, brides / Bereft, and tender hearts of sisters grieving, / Orphaned boys – all cursed the war."[43]

Even in the underworld we cannot escape the mourning and the recitation of mourning to the dead. In the last book of *The Odyssey*, Agamémnon describes the death of Akhilleus We carried you down to the ships, bathed your body with warm water and scented oil; officers wept hot tears. Your mother Thetis came with nereids lamenting. The Muses sang a threnody. After seventeen days and nights we put you on the pyre. Your bones are mixed with Patróklos'.[44]

In the late eighteenth and nineteenth centuries, the two realms, private and public, the individual and the community, the historical and the transcendental, had become worthy opponents of one another and dynamic enough to offer, in the novel, choices and changes, new plots and problems, a variety of solutions, which make that genre, as it bores inward, seem ironically less confining than the epic with its broad sweep. And if we look at a novelist with epic visions, we have only to keep in mind how dynamically Zola treats the dialectic between the public and private worlds in *La Débacle* or for that matter, Tolstoy in *War and Peace*, to understand how single-minded *The Iliad* is, as grey-eyed Athêna stirs the attack, "and each man in his heart / grew strong to fight and never quit...for at her passage war itself became / lovelier than return, lovelier than sailing / ...to their own native land."[45]

One may argue that *The Odyssey* is as much a picaresque tale or a romance as an epic – George Sarton calls it the world's first novel – and the desire for a return home might seem not just a nostalgic wish but a guiding and formal shaping of the travels. One may argue as well that the linear line of time begins with the end of the war and ends with the arrival home. Odysseus prays for Nausicca that she may have a home, a husband, harmonious converse, "the best thing in the world / being a strong house held in serenity / where man and wife agree...," for King Alkinoös, that he be settled in his land giving joy to wives and children in a realm free from woe, and for himself that god would grant him, after his voyage, his own wife and those he loves safe and sound.[46]

But we have seen in Thucydides that when the public invades the private realm there is hell to pay. The "great wanderer come home"[47] is destined to have an arrival more typical of the epic than the picaresque novel as he brings the battlefield into domestic halls, where the slaughter covers the walls and floors with the blood of the suitors' chopped off noses and ears, pulled off genitals, (fed to the dogs), and hacked off hands and feet. Oh, Penélopè, you should have seen him, Eurykleia gushes, there was Odysseus, in the midst of the floor littered with dead bodies, "a lion / splashed with mire and blood."[48] It would have made you proud. We are reminded of the exchange on Death in another context between Trim and Obadiah in *Tristram Shandy*: " – He's nothing, Obadiah, at all in the field. – But he's very frightful in a house...."[49]

After the particularly gruesome killings, and the replenishment of his flocks through raids, Odysseus is allowed to settle into a Shakespearean ending directed by the Prospero-like gods. Zeus instructs Athêna with a kind of nonchalance, to

> Conclude it as you will.
> There is one proper way, if I may say so:
> Odysseus' honor being satisfied,
> let him be king by a sworn pact forever,
> and we, for our part, will blot out the memory
> of sons and brothers slain. As in the old time
> let men of Ithaka henceforth be friends;
> prosperity enough, and peace attend them.[50]

Once he is safely home, all passion spent, neither the epic nor the

Gods are interested in him. The Gods, in fact, may sense that they will disappear with the epic. Let Teirêsias have the last prophetic word about the hero's soft seaborne death in "rich old age, / your country folk in blessed peace around you."[51]

Ithaca is a city to which the hero can return, that very hero known as "the wily raider of cities." How happy he was we can only guess. Tennyson had his own ideas on the subject. And so did Fermina Daza in Gabriel García Márquez's *Love in the Time of Cholera*: "The problem in public life is learning to overcome terror; the problem in married life is learning to overcome boredom."[52]

Virgil's *Aeneid* is a different kind of epic, as it dwells not on the destruction of the city Aeneas has left but on the founding of new cities, with their doors opening to the private realm. Throughout this work we feel a brake on belligerent desires, though Aeneas does his share of fighting. Even in the canonical journey to the underworld there is a special kind of heaven for those who were not warriors so much as founders of cities,[53] bettering life by discovering new truths and skills, making themselves remembered by benefactions.

When Aeneas looks over Carthage, pillage and plunder are far from his mind. Though romance soon moves dramatically into the picture, he seems as interested in Carthage as in Dido, marveling at a city working to construct itself, walls, dwellings, buildings, roads, a citadel, harbors, theatres etc. Laws are being enacted, magistrates and a senate chosen. Zeus sends Mercury to pull Aeneas away from his lover not because he must destroy a city but because he is to "bring the whole world under law's dominion."[54]

And Aeneas is not the founder of only one city. On the way to his destination, he stops at "the ancient land of the Curetës," where he is eager to build another Troy called Pergamum. He urges those of his party who wish to stay to "love their new-found hearths," engage in marriage, sow new fields, while he gives out homesteads and laws. Another settlement along the way, with quarters called Illium and Troy, reversing destruction, is laid down with home sites and boundaries, laws and assemblies. "All had one thing to say: a town and home / Were what they dreamed of...."[55]

The ur ex-pat hero passes through the world to his promised new land, but this is not an alien, plotless world through which he travels; it is one of sacred places once peopled, that carry tales.

> Near the cold stream of Caerë there's a grove
> Immense and deep, awesome to our forebears
> The hills encircle it with dark fir trees
> The tale goes etc.

or

> ...Marveling,
> Aeneas gladly looked at all about him,
> Delighted with the setting, asking questions,
> Hearing of earlier men and what they left.
> Then King Evander, founder unaware
> Of Rome's great citadel, said:
> "These woodland places
> Once were homes of local fauns and nymphs
> Together with a race of men that came
> From tree trunks, from hard oak:..."[56]

Virgil's sense of place prefigures the novel.

An Epic Loss of Will

Unlike the narrative of the novel, which dotes on secrets, that of the epic is a give-away, its gods, of necessity, arch story spoilers and blabber mouths (the champion being Jupiter, who tells Venus exactly what's going to happen in a package of three centuries!).[1] Through the voice of a horse, Hera informs Akhilleus what he is cognizant of already. "Why prophesy my death? No need. / What is in store for me I know, know well: / to die here, far away from my dear father, / my mother, too."[2] Previously, he had been forced by his mother to tiresomely rehearse his fate. When the immortal Thetis asks her son why he is weeping he answers "Why tell you what you know,"[2] and then proceeds to tell her what she knows because we have to know what we already know.

The recitations of fate are guaranteed in part by human nature but it is the absence of will which dooms the epic characters to repeat history. Hektor will kill Patróklos, and enraged, Akhilleus will slay Hektor, Zeus tells a chastened Hera and the reader or, more to the point, the listener, in one of the many examples of bean-spilling. "...From that moment / I'll turn the tide of battle on the beach / decisively, once and for all, / until the Akhaians capture Ilion, / as Athêna planned and willed it. But until / that killing I shall not remit my wrath..."[3]

We know that when an arrow is thrown, a god sees to it that it reaches or fails to reach its intended target. All the gods' tools, their nimbuses, their superb out-patient surgery, simply prolong the appointed moment as well. Twice Athêna makes Odysseus "seem / taller, and massive too, with crisping hair / in curls like petals of wild hyacinth /, but all red-golden." Not to neglect the matching Penélopè, Athêna gives her an extreme make-over while she sleeps – "With ambrosia / she bathed her cheeks and throat and smoothed her brow... Grandeur she gave her, too, in height and form, / and made her whiter than carved ivory."[4] Even Odysseus' father has his turn, the goddess filling out his limbs, restoring his girth and stature of old. (Though all this is no match for the disguises of the gods themselves.)

From the very beginning of *The Iliad*, when the private story of Akhilleus' anger and the grief it causes is touched on, any subjective examination is closed off – "the will of Zeus was done." The personal interior experience, according to Lukács "remains inside the subject: it becomes mood." Which is another way of saying there is no "antagonistic duality of soul and world" in the hero.[5] "The men of Homer," Ortega writes, "belong to the same world as their desires."[6] They do not reform or make over, they do not give up the habitual, they simply endure.

But what is the point in developing an intricate emotional texture when Zeus can stir Patróklos' heart to fury.[7] Not to worry as well whether one's courage will be adequate to the matter, for "Strongest of all... is the mind of Zeus / who... can turn back / a champion, and rob him of triumph, / even when he incites the man,"[8] which says a lot about his perversity, as well. Akhilleus tells Agamémnon to look at those men lying dead "whom Hektor killed when Zeus allowed him glory...."[9] But however sure-footed and swift, Hektor speeds on the chariots "at the god's command."[10] And "It was not given to Odysseus / to finish off Sarpêdôn, but Athêna / turned his fury upon the Lykians."[11]

Homer's heroes are hardly self-generating. So why are they heroes at all? Hektor himself admits his shortcomings. Though he hasn't always shown courage,[12] he will not run away from Akhilleus now, as he had done before, reluctant to face him. ("A man might be a coward at one time," Parson Adams says in *Joseph Andrews*, "and brave at another...Paris fights and Hector runs away.")[13] Glaukos calls Hektor "a great man" by his looks, "but in a fight you are far from great... a big name, and a craven!"[14] The unheroic truth is, he needs constant nudging. Apollo, at Hektor's elbow in the guise of a good foreign friend, asks: "Would any Akhaian / fear you now? How openly you shrank / from Meneláos – in the past, at least, no tough man with a spear!"[15] Still, the die has been cast long ago. Priam, who has lost so many children already, begs Hektor, his pride and joy, to spare him the agony of losing him by refusing to fight with Akhilleus, but his pleas fall on necessarily deaf ears.[16]

Akhilleus is called noble and brave, though his selfish moping confirms the result Wiglaf notes in *Beowulf*: "Often when one man follows his own will / many are hurt."[17] Besides, who couldn't have been a hero with a little help from his friends. "No man can fight Akhilleus! / In every battle," complains Aeneas, "one of the gods is there / to save him from destruction, while his weapon / flies unwavering till it bites its way / thru some man's flesh."[18]

"O grey-eyed one, fire my heart and brace me," Odysseus prays to Athêna, who has given him his gift of self-possession and courage. "I'll take on fighting men three strong / if you fight at my back, immortal lady!",[19] and she obliges when she tells the returned Odysseus that as his goddess-guardian, "if fifty bands of men surrounded us / and every sword sang for your blood / you could make off still with their cows and sheep."[20] Aeneas has but to give the Prophetess (Sibyl) his prayers, the seer tells him, and she will inform him of the way to avoid "Each difficulty, or face it. Do her reverence / And she will bring you through."[21]

The gods are doubly potent because the end always justifies the means. Athêna can give Diomêdês "nimbleness in the legs, sure feet and hands" when he prays to her, but if he should still come up short, she sees to it by hook or crook he wins.[22] When Odysseus prays to Athêna to help him beat Aías and Pallas, she lightens his legs and trips Aías on the dead run at the finish line where ox dung has dropped, plugging Aías' mouth and nose with muck, her version of extreme sport.[22]

We do not doubt for a moment that, whatever the gods decide, the epic heroes will turn full face to destiny with a kind of dumb nobility. They simply have no choice in the matter. If the Akhaians are slated to win, still, at one time or another in the long battles, "A fool would know / that Zeus had thrown his weight behind the Trojans...."[23] But Aías and Meneláos, who were not blind, behave as they have always behaved and as they always will behave. By the time we get to an epic like *Beowulf*, Fate can be helped along "by the daring of one man," though there is still a kind of touching all the bases about it: "Often, for undaunted courage, / fate spares the man it has not already marked."[24]

What complicates matters in the classical epic is that the inhabitants of Mt. Olympus, who seem to have the control of mankind's fate, turn out to live in a world whose transcendence is continually marred by their well-known less than heavenly actions and emotions which they are programmed by category to act out. Zeus cannot prevent his own son, Sarpêdôn, from dying undefended. And, as we are well aware, there is nothing superior about the character of the gods. Zeus calls Hera "eternal bitch"[25] for her underhanded work, and moving to the Roman world, Venus complains to Neptune that Juno's anger drives her "to prayers beneath [her] dignity."[26] More to the point are the words of Dîonê: "Many of us who live upon Olympos / have taken hurt from men, and hurt each other."[27]

The city of the gods persuades us no more than Pericles' shining city on the hill, and, as a product of man's imagination, why should it. After Athêna gives directions to Nausikaa, the goddess departs for Olympos, where, as men say, there is "Never a tremor of wind, or a splash of rain, / no errant snowflake comes to stain that heaven, / so calm, so vaporless, the world of light."[28]

Still, the gods, like Pericles, try to make a good case. Apollo saves Aeneas from being killed by Diomêdês, then cries "Look out! Give way!

/ enough of this, this craze to vie with gods! / Our kind, immortals of the open sky, / will never be like yours, earth-faring men."[29] Poseiden asks why, being so much more powerful than man, the gods should become embroiled in war. Better to move away from "the trampled plain and take / some lookout post on high. Let man make war!"[30]

But even in moments of seeming transcendence, the gods are full of ungodly sadistic satisfaction : "In his chair / withdrawn from all, [Zeus] gloried, looking down / on wall and ship and metal flash of battle, / men slaying others, and the quiet slain," or condescension: "For of all creatures that breathe and move on earth, none is more to be pitied than a man."[31] There may be "only Trojans and Akhaians ... left now in the great fight on the plain,"[32] but there is little distinction or dialectic between a real world and an ideal one. (Imagine a bumper sticker asking what Hera would have done.)

The divinities, like earthly kings, have to jealously guard their portion of the Olympic domain and the distinctive characteristic which belongs to them. But Fortune, Fate, Moira is the uncorrupted power above the Gods, and it has a long rule. In *The Aeneid*, we feel its power when Aeneas comes to his destination "as one ordained, / Brought by palpable will of the unseen."[33] And Fortune, that prevails in everything, has brought King Evander to his land as well.[34] Fate even steps on the toes of the early Christian divinity in *Beowulf*: "So may a man not marked by fate / easily escape exile and woe / by the grace of God."[35]

Thucydides lived at a time when the old religion was fading (we remember growing accusations by a fearful culture against the "impious" such as Alcibiades, Pericles, Aspasia, Socrates) and in 438 a bill providing that "those who do not believe in the gods...should be impeached"[36] was introduced. But though a new religion of moral precepts was not yet in view, Realpolitik ruled. While the Athenians argue to an assembly of regional groups at Sparta before the conflict that war is simply an affair of accident and chance from which we are not exempt,[37] the Melians imagine, at a later time, that the gods will support them because they are just men fighting against the unjust and deserve as much good fortune as the Athenians. (They should be careful what they wish for. If the twentieth century has taught us anything, it is that being God's "chosen people" is no picnic.) To which the Athenians answer: "When you speak of the favor of the gods, we may fairly hope for that as yourselves; neither our pretensions nor our conduct being in any way contrary to what men believe of the gods, or practice among themselves. Of the gods we believe, and of men we know, that by a necessary law of their nature they rule wherever they can."[38] We believe the gods rule wherever they can is hardly reassuring.

Nevertheless, they are decidedly convenient. Since neither the epic characters nor their gods have any need to take moral responsibility for their actions – a world that calls for moral imagination will have to wait for a different mode of literature – there is little self-blame in evidence, a sure sign of moral insensitivity. Aeneas can extricate himself from a sticky love affair by blaming it all on the gods. Please, no more appeals that inflame the heart, Dido. I sail for Italy "not of my own free will."[39] It is interesting to recall the story of his father Anchises in this regard, who was seduced by Aphrodite, herself made to fall in love by Zeus. And Aphrodite, in turn, injects passion into him. The upshot of all this engineered passion is the birth of Aeneas, but nothing comes free, especially free will, and for the privilege of siring such a son, Anchises will pay with feebleness and premature old age, because, after all, fair is fair; though he was forced to do so, he has committed a sacrilege.[40]

We might hope for a breaking out as Akhilleus momentarily wonders if it was "better for us / in any way, when we were sore at heart, / to waste ourselves in strife over a girl,"[41] but it turns out to be the fault of Father Zeus, who sends "mankind / prodigious follies. Never otherwise / had Agamémnon stung me through and through; / never would he have been so empty-headed / as to defy my will and take the girl!"[42] Nor is Agamémnon about to step up to the plate. "But I am not to blame. / Zeus and Fate and a nightmare Fury are, for putting savage Folly in my mind /...when I wrested Akhilleus' prize of war from him. In truth, / what could I do? Divine will shapes these things. Ruinous Folly, eldest daughter of Zeus / beguiles us all."[43]

Priam's entire family is brought down by the irresistible beauty of Helen, (Aeneas considers the punishment suffered by Priam's house unmerited),[44] but the king has no inclination to blame her or his son;

clearly, he is not inclined to blame anyone but the gods "for bringing on / this war against the Akhaians, to our sorrow."⁴⁵ And Aeneas, given shelter by Dido, asks the gods to reward her, though with his characteristic uncertainty, for "surely there are powers that care for goodness, / Surely somewhere justice counts."⁴⁶ In a step forward, he even acknowledges that she must be already rewarded by her consciousness of acting well. Still, in *The Odyssey*, the gods send the ball back over the net, keeping the game moving from side to side, but never forward, in typical epic fashion. "My word, how mortals take the gods to task!/ All their afflictions come from us, we hear./ And what of their own failings? Greed and folly / double the suffering in the lot of man."⁴⁷ Finally, in a beautiful tautology, the god of war and his consort are blamed for "the shameless butchery of war."⁴⁸ The moral imagination of the story is going nowhere fast.

Nor are Thucydides' Athenians inclined to self-examination. When they had listened to the recital of the disaster in Sicily, they "were angry with the orators who had joined in promoting the expedition, just as if they had not themselves voted it, and were enraged with the reciters of oracles and soothsayers, and all other omenmongers of the time" who had become more powerful since the plague, for encouraging "them to hope that they should conquer Sicily."⁴⁹

The epic characters seem to have, in general, an untroubled relationship with the gods, but if the possibilities of moral responsibility, empathic imagination and good reading, which could open the door of the epic prison, begin in doubt about the unique power of the gods, fate and prognosticators, then there are small stirrings along the way, even in Homer. Telémakhos expresses skepticism about his father's return: "It could not be – even if the gods willed it." Whereupon Athêna answers: "What strange talk you permit yourself, Telémakhos. / A god could save the man by simply wishing it / from the farthest shore in the world."⁵⁰ Aeneas has similar doubts. Wondering to his mother Venus if he is truly destined to go through insecurities and dangers without harm, he asks: "Which of the gods can wield that power?"⁵¹ And though Agamémnon is willing to sacrifice his daughter for smooth sailing, Hektor vows to fight for his country whether birds fly right or left.⁵²

After reading what he deems a sign from heaven, Anchises lifts his hands and voice in joy: "Omnipotent Jupiter, if prayers affect you, / Look down upon us, that is all I ask, / If by devotion to the gods we earn it, / Grant us a new sign and confirm this portent!"[53] Fortunately, a star falls for him, but who can blame him for his uncertainty. We saw what little effect Odysseus' offer of a ram had on Zeus,[54] who allows his ships to be destroyed and his companions to be killed. Everywhere in Virgil there are questions, even by the poet himself. "Who could describe that carnage in a song…Was it thy pleasure, Jupiter, that peoples / Afterward to live in lasting peace / Should rend each other in so black a storm?"[55]

Ritual offers security when a once vibrant belief has weakened. Aeneas tries to persuade the Arcadian King Evander to come over to his side and traces their common ancestry, (with some skepticism). The Father of your line, he tells him, was Mercury whom Maia bore, "Fathered, if we can trust these tales, / By that same Atlas, pillar of starry sky,"[56] but King Evander will have none of that "empty-headed superstition…we carry out these rites, / Renewed each year, as men saved from barbaric / Dangers in the past."[57]

We might be tempted to view these sentiments as novelistic precursors were it not for the divine intervention in Dido's passion for Aeneas,[58] that most personal of emotions. And the hero is kept moving by a destiny given him from above. The significant move is from the battlefield to romance, from the public to the private, from the Olympic gods to the *lares* and *penates*. Greek households did have their own religious centers and ceremonies, though they play no role in Homeric epics, but there is a real shift to private gods when we come to *The Aeneid*. (Offerings to divinities who live in the house were more often bits of daily food,[59] a lot easier on the digestive system than the previous huge chunks of choice goats or sheep.)

The domestic gods watch over Aeneas while he sleeps, comfort him and hint at a kind of private spirituality. Many a bloody battle will have to be gotten through before and after Aeneas will lie down by the river and be told by the god Tibernus "Here is your home, your hearth gods, fixed and sure. /... Angers that rose / Among the gods have passed."[60] *The Aeneid* has that domestic air about it so necessary for the novel. Already, as Aeneas leaves Troy, he asks his father to carry the hearth gods while he purges himself of public life. "It would be wrong for me to handle them -/ Just come from such hard fighting, bloody work-/ Until I wash myself in running water."[61]

The Seer tells Aeneas and his company to keep hold of their ritual, and insist that their progeny remain religiously pure. And when saying prayers, one must not be unsettled by omens.[62] But the emphasis is on familial duties. Aeneas' pietas, though he is the son of a goddess, does not require him to leave his father and go off to war once more, like Priam's sons, (though he will have to fight in order to reach the promised land), but rather makes him responsible for his care, just as the well-being of Aeneas' son Ascanius, (Iulius) depends, he later declares, wholly on his father's return from adventure.[63] But this new world brings to its inhabitants a significant will that encounters the challenge of choice.

An Epic Failure of Empathic Imagination

When Lykáôn, Priam's son, is threatened by death at the hands of Akhilleus, he begs for mercy. Akhilleus admits that he might have spared him before Patróklos was killed, but surely not now and surely not Priam's son. Yet when he expands into philosophical recognition, when we, brought up on novels, might hope that the fate of all mankind leads him to mercy, to surcease of war, to recognition, he cannot think of anything more to say except "Come, friend, face your death" as he, however large, handsome, noble and divine, must as well. "A morning comes or evening or high noon / when someone takes my life away in war, / a spear-cast, or an arrow from a bow string."[1] (These heroes of destiny never make the mistake the acquaintances of Ivan Ilyich do in comforting themselves with the realization that "he's dead but I'm alive!")[2] Everything to be endured, nothing to be learned.

Akhilleus is utterly straightforward with the grief-stricken Priam: "This is the way / the gods ordained the destiny of men, / to bear such burdens in our lives, while they / feel no affliction…Endure it, then, and do not mourn forever / for your dead son. There is no remedy. / You will not make him stand again. Rather, / await some new misfortune to be suffered."³ The virility involved in accepting one's fate and of fighting with courage, of finding it beautiful to meet death in arms, is not Lukács' mature virility of the novel but, as Schiller calls it, the naïveté of the epic.⁴

Full of detail as Homer's stories are, the outlook for his heroes is as spare as any hero without psychology or a significant self-consciousness must be. (Interestingly, the hyper self-consciousness of the private modern protagonist, on view in memoirs, solipsistic narratives and game novels creates the same psychic stasis, the same absence of dialectical drama, in an entirely different world from the epic, but on a stage as decidedly private as Homer's is public.)

Akhilleus knows he is the hero of his story and he knows how it will end, but David Copperfield, who knows he is in the story he tells, is uncertain whether he will turn out to be the hero of his own life or whether "that station will be held by anybody else." And uncertain, as well, though he is the narrator, how his story will end, for he must grow to accommodate and earn that ending. In fact, he does not know who he is until his story develops, whereas Akhilleus and Hector and the Athenian citizen are never uncertain from the day they are born. Suffering is recognized as a teacher more often in the classic tragedies of public and private balance – (the chorus in Aeschylus' "Agamémnon" tells us that wisdom, though given by Zeus, comes through suffering)⁵ – than in the epic world. A rare exception is Dido, who learns through pain how to comfort those who suffer.⁶

Odysseus is allowed more room for his cunning in the picaresque form his epic takes than he had in *The Iliad*. Indeed, for many pages of *The Odyssey*, he is, as his own narrator and protagonist, the equal of blind Homer and of the blind minstrel of Alkinoos' court. "You speak with art," the king tells him, "You told as a poet would, a man who knows the world."⁷ Other epics have changing narrators for short periods of time, but Odysseus is allotted one sixth of his book. Still, even this infinitely resourceful storyteller who found his tricky way into Troy cannot nor wants to find a way out of the epic. He accepts the lot Zeus has given him, "danger and war / to wind upon the spindle of our years / until we die to the last man."⁸ There is no remorse or self-questioning.

Some say that Odysseus is wiser at the end of his journeys than he is at the beginning,[9] but I see little evidence of that. Dante's "Ulysses" opens up a novelistic desire in his famous confession:

> not sweetness of a son, not reverence
> for an aging father, not the debt of love
> I owed Penélopè to make her happy,
> could quench deep in myself the burning wish
> to know the world and have experience
> of all men's vices, of all human worth...
>
> Consider what you came from: you are Greeks!
> You were not born to live like mindless brutes
> but to follow paths of excellence and knowledge.[10]

Tennyson shows us a more passive hero, who nevertheless feels it is "not too late to seek a newer world,"[11] though still a distance from the novelistic Stephen Daedalus who goes out into the world "to forge in the smithy of my soul the uncreated conscience of my race."[12] The fact of the matter is that though Homer's Odysseus has had many adventures, mythic and lyrical, there is no other world to go to. The conscience of his race is immanent in the epic. The hero remains a stranger to "the real torment of seeking and the real danger of finding."[13] The Odysseus who returns to Ithaca an old man differs from the vigorous one who left the Trojan battlefield only in age.

Nor is Akhilleus wiser even in the underworld, though we entertain some glimmer of hope when Odysseus finds him there, the great hero complaining that he would rather have been a farm hand on earth than "lord it over all the exhausted dead."[14] But his next question slams the epic door shut. "Tell me, what news of the prince my son, did he / come after me to make a name in battle / or could it be he did not? Do you know if rank and honor still belong to Pêleus / in the towns of the Myrmidons?" The only thing he seems to regret is that he can no longer help his father because he is no longer the man he was "in those days / when I made bastion for the Argives / and put an army's best men in the dust."[15]

After Akhilleus mercilessly kills Priam's son Lykáôn, who has begged for mercy, he launches into a philosophical riff about the destiny of all men, then takes his victim by the foot and slings him down river, enjoying the notion that his mother will not be able to put him on his bed to mourn over him, an epic pattern we have seen before.[16]

Priam has lost his best sons in the war and now he must depend upon those sons whom he calls "poltroons," "hollow men," "dancers", "light-fingered pillagers of lambs and kids from the town pens," those sons who dread" the rough edge of their father's tongue," to prepare a cart for Hektor's body.[17] But for all his sorrow, he remains fixated on himself, imagining that the "most harrowing / of all that men in their hard lives endure" would be for an old man to fall and for dogs to disfigure his grey head, cheek and genitals.[18]

Odysseus shows that fatal disjunction of the epic, used so powerfully in Dickens' novels – see Jo in *Bleak House* – weeping such piteous tears over a minstrel's song about the destruction of Troy[19] that Alkínöos asks why, being on the victorious side, he weeps. Did you lose some kin, some dear friends? We never know whether it is his companions he mourns or the destruction of a city and its inhabitants. Perhaps he is on the cusp of universality; but when he becomes the narrator, he blithely talks about killing men and plundering and enslaving the women.[20]

Hektor displays some self-awareness when he realizes that his vanity has led him into trouble – "troops have perished for my foolish pride, / I am ashamed to face townsmen and women"[21] – but his solutions are limited to his epic plot: better when the crunch comes, "that I appear as he who killed Akhilleus / man to man, or else that I went down / before him honorably for the city's sake."[21] Akhilleus' vanity has led to Patróklos' death and he too exhibits some self-consciousness. After his mother, Thetis, tells him in typical story-spoiling fashion that he is to die soon after Hektor, he understands what his brooding has wrought and is able to let go of his anger against Agamémmnon, but has he had an epiphany?

So it might seem, and he is no mean poet in expressing his feelings here: "Ai! let strife and rancor / perish from the lives of gods and men, / with anger that envenoms even the wise / and is far sweeter than slow-dripping honey, / clouding the hearts of men like smoke."[22] But only a few lines down the page here he is again: "Now, though, may I win my perfect glory / and make some wife of Troy break down, / or some deep-breasted Dardan woman sob / and wipe tears from her soft cheeks. They'll know then / how long they had been spared the deaths of men / while I abstained from war,"[23] and in a later Marlovian rant he confesses that "slaughter and blood are what I crave and groans / of anguished men!"[24]

Zeus assures his messenger Iris that Akhilleus is "no madman, / but dutiful toward men who beg his mercy."[25] Hektor, at the point of death, perceives his nemesis more clearly than the number one God: "I see you now for what you are. No chance / to win you over. Iron in your breast/ your heart is."[26] Hektor begs for his body to be sent back to his parents, and Akhilleus answers: "Beg me no beggary by soul or parents, / whining dog! Would god my passion drove me / to slaughter you and eat you raw, you've caused / such agony to me!"[27]

As Priam brings himself to kiss the very hand that killed his son, he hopes that when Akhilleus sees him as an old father, he will make the connection with his own father and show pity. While Hektor has been surrounded by family, Akhilleus has always been a singularly lonely figure, an only child brooding in his tent. By begging for one son, though he has lost other sons at the hands of his tormenter, Priam sharpens the analogue. And it seems to be working. The old man has stirred images of Akhilleus' own father in his mind, "an ache of grief."[28] Gently, he puts Priam's hand aside.

Both men naturally fall into their own sorrows "as they remembered: the old king huddled at Akhilleus's feet / wept, and wept for Hektor, killer of men, / while great Akhilleus wept for his own father / as for Patróklos once again, and sobbing / filled the room."[29] Encased in their own private sorrow as they are, we hope, nevertheless, for a reaching out in the softened atmosphere. "Akhilleus spoke in a warm rush of words:...'We'll probe our wounds no more but let them rest, / though grief lies heavy on us. Tears heal nothing.'"[30] And we know full well that in Homer's world, they don't. But as soon as Priam dares ask for the body of his son, the magic moment is over. "Do not vex me, sir,"

Akhilleus snaps, "I have intended, in my own good time, to yield up Hektor to you... Therefore, let me be: / sting my sore heart again, and even here, / under my own roof, suppliant though you are, / I may not spare you, sir, but trample on / the express command of Zeus."[31]

Akhilleus is not inclined to give Priam the tortured body of his son though he himself knows full well that he will not live long for his mother Thetis or a grieving father. Priam's sin is to have come close to being successful in drawing Akhilleus out of himself. We cannot say what the Greek hero feels at this moment; there is always that uncrossed barrier.

We have become accustomed to the fact that there is no real empathy or vision on either side. The Akhaians "hastened round to see / Hektor's fine body and his comely face, / and no one came who did not stab the body."[32] Hektor's body, which Akhilleus has treated with "shameless abuse"[33] – he has been told of Zeus' anger because he had not returned the body to Priam – is put on a cart that will be pulled home. Only when we have lost all hope for some kind of recognition, the clouds part for an instant in the most extraordinary moment of this extraordinary epic. After all the speeches, the feasting is done, the old man and the young one truly see each other for an instant, that true vision which is the foundation of the novel's empathic imagination. "Priam, the heir of Dárdanos, gazed long / in wonder at Akhilleus' form and scale – so like the gods in aspect. And Akhilleus / in his turn gazed in wonder upon Priam, / royal in visage as in speech."[34] The younger man promises to hold off from attack until the allotted days agreed upon for Hektor's funeral are over. And then the slaughter will resume.

Sanity and Slaughter

In *The Iliad*, Glaukos tells us eloquently that the generations of men are like leaves upon the earth, "old leaves, cast on the ground by wind, young leaves / the greening forest bears when spring comes in. / So mortals pass; one generation flowers / even as another dies away."[1]

Pericles and his Athenians find this constant renewal of young resources reassuring. The war is about to begin in earnest. "And if both sides nourished the boldest hopes and put forth their utmost strength for the war, this was only natural. Zeal is always at its height at the commencement of an undertaking; and on this particular occasion the Peloponnesus and Athens were both full of young men whose inexperience made them eager to take up arms...."[2]

But by the seventeenth year of the war, Nicias, chosen, against his will, to command Athenian troops for an invasion of Sicily, has words of caution, arguing that such an expedition, upon such a slight and specious pretext, would be ill-advised. We have enough on our hands with Sparta. Besides, we have just recovered from plague and war; we should use our down time wisely. Our older men, who know the vagaries of fortune, should keep the eager young from such an enterprise.[3]

The lifting of the plague and the peace that had reigned for a time, however, had allowed a number of males to reach manhood and capital to accumulate. Time to throw new forces into the fields. Alcibiades had whipped up the enthusiasm of his listeners with the certainty of future conquest, the growth of Athenian prestige, and the excitement of adventure.[4]

Though the cautious Nicias sees a more troubling picture, in the perversity of intention, the audience grows simply more eager than ever to take up the expedition. The older among them thought they would have no trouble against the enemy with so overwhelming a force, while the younger felt the longing characteristic of those in the prime of life for foreign sights and shores, never doubting they would come home safely. ("Fighting side by side with a companion is far nicer than fighting alone. Each encourages the other and the feeling of having an enemy and that of having a friend fuse in similar warmth," Italo Calvino's Raimbaut remarks.)[5] Meanwhile, the common people and the soldiers were eager to earn wages and to establish a steady flow of income into the future.[6]

Once the disgraced and defeated Athenians try to leave Sicily, it is impossible not to contrast "the splendor and glory of their setting out with the humiliation in which the adventure had ended."[7] (At the beginning of the First World War young men marched off on either side, hardly understanding why, not even wanting to know why, egged on by the cheers of women, the joy of camaraderie, the promise of a wider world, only to end their lives in narrow muddy trenches. By the end of this war, half the British infantry was younger than nineteen).

When history could no longer be served by the epic form, it eventually found, as we have seen, a home in the novel, notwithstanding the persuasive observation of Lukács that the novel had lost its bearings in the universe. There history became a powerful dialectical force against the private and spiritual realms in a world where characters were free to forge their own fates. But eventually, history outgrew and sabotaged its creative role and burst its bounds to rage free, leaving us with the knowledge that the novel could not change human nature "by an inch or an ounce."

In the first battle of the Somme, of the 110,000 who attacked the Germans, 60,000 British were killed in one day. The Allied offensive forced Germans to slacken their pressure, but the French took 380,000 casualties (162,000 dead), the Germans 330,000 (143,000 dead), blown to pieces, left to rot, vanished in mud or rubble or crippled for life. At Verdun, 542,000 French perished, 434,000 Germans. After the heavy allied bombardment had churned up the ground at Passchendaele, many of the 370,000 British, sick and frozen, drowned in the mud[8] as the Athenians had drowned in the Assinarus River. By the end of a war to end all wars, three and a half million of the enemy had been slaughtered or died of disease and misery, five million of the allies. And that was just the beginning of the twentieth century.

We all recall that on the first Christmas Day of World War I, a temporary truce was declared, during which the British and the Germans in the trenches met in No Man's Land, a cosmic field if ever there was one, to exchange cigarettes and take snapshots, and on Christmas of 1915 the opposing sides played a game of soccer.[9] Such moments of sanity in every war simply intensify the incessant rhythm when it returns. Not very far into battle, Homer tells us, Paris suggests that Hektor and Meneláos should fight it out, the others laying down their arms – "Now all hearts lifted at his words, for both sides / hoped for an end of miserable war...."[10] Later, Aiás Telamônios and Hektor, each fighting as a representative of his side, break off their duel at the suggestion of others, allowing afterwards the opposing forces to say: "These two fought and gave no quarter / in close combat, yet they parted friends."¹¹ Diomêdês discovers a connection to the Trojan Glaukos on the battlefield: "Why / you are my friend! My grandfather, Oineus, / made friends of us long years ago. He welcomed / Prince Bellérophontês in his hall / his guest for twenty days." They then exchange battle-gear and inform all around them of "this bond of friendship from our fathers."¹²

The sigh of Sarpêdon to Glaukos on the Homeric stage has a universal ring. "Ah, cousin, could we but survive this war / to live forever deathless, without age, / I would not ever go again to battle, / nor would I send you there for honor's sake!" But history's nightmare goes on: "now a thousand shapes of death surround us, / and no man can escape them, or be safe. / Let us attack – whether to give some fellow / glory or to win it from him."¹³

The epic war, which cannot be stopped, has had to find a new form with the advent of television as it becomes performance art, assuming, once again, the public characteristics of a Thucydidian history, reporters embedded with the troops taking on the narrative. And a Bardic art as well. Each disaster carries its own musical theme of introduction, echoing the minstrel's harp and the old war chants. If the universality of the television world should be conducive to a deeper fellow feeling, the screen also shows what Stanley Cavell calls "the growing uninhabitablity of the world,"¹⁴ and encourages in us a loss of will. We have, in a way, finally become if not, in William James' phrase, cosmic readers, at least cosmic viewers. We may have been banished from the world of Homer, where "life and meaning were present with perfect immanence in every manifestation of life,"¹⁵ banished as well from our transcendental home, but we find a form which we thought we had left behind revitalized as we enter our world of the absurd, our world where blame is never assumed, where patterns cannot change, a world in which we are forced to watch as well as listen to the epic and its stubborn human nature in full flower. Whatever world we live in, we cannot spring open the prison gates.

How the Novel Got Its Game

The House of Fiction

IT WAS JUST A MATTER of luck that I landed on the far end of a cultural line featuring the world's great novels of (dare I say it) moral imagination. Those who came up short at the beginning of the run still had, of course, the compensation of *Don Quixote*, whose protagonist was too modest when he called the age and century in which his famous exploits would be published happy.[1] Happy indeed all the ages to follow which paid homage to the progenitor of these novels.

It is a commonplace that every novel after *Don Quixote* is derived from it and carries its central polarities and forms. Fielding makes no bones about the fact that *Joseph Andrews* was "written in Imitation of the Manner of Cervantes" by announcing it on the title page, and he provides, in the adventures of Parson Adams, the requisite inns and magical apparitions.[2] Laurence Sterne is equally devoted to Cervantes. Tristram's Yorick rides a horse thinner than Rocinante, suffers blows to the head like Sancho Panza, speaks on his death bed in cervantick tones, and has qualities which come "up to any of the honest refinements of the peerless knight of La Mancha, whom, by the bye, with all his follies, I love more, and would actually have gone farther to have paid a visit to, than the greatest hero of antiquity."[3]

Those who have come upon the scene after the end of the great flowering still hold, of course, the option of taking a trip through the novels of Austen, Dickens, Conrad, Tolstoy, Dostoevsky, George Eliot and company. But the summer afternoons which Henry James called the two most beautiful words in the English language not only for their umbrageous teas but also for the comfortable opportunity they provided to read his works in a private world, no longer exist. We are left wishing, like a character in Italo Calvino's *If on a winter's night a traveler* that we could rediscover that innocent, almost primitive condition of natural reading which we had taken for granted.[4]

Milan Kundera complains, strangely I think – *Don Quixote* alone gives the lie to his observation – that through the years the novel hasn't taken much advantage of its Protean powers, its almost boundless freedom.[5] But Fielding writes in his preface he is doing something in *Joseph Andrews* he does not remember to have seen "hitherto attempted in our language." Sterne's Tristram Shandy wants us to know that "in writing what I have set about, I shall confine myself neither to [Horace's] rules, nor to any man's rules that ever lived,"[6] though he borrows a little bit of razzle-dazzle from Fielding who introduced matter in *Joseph Andrews* "for no other purpose than to lengthen out a short chapter...."[7] Sterne inspires Diderot to go so far as to proclaim that his *Jacques le fataliste* is, in fact, not a novel. Flaubert writes a new kind of novel in 1860, Proust in 1910, and James Joyce's *Ulysses* sees the light of day in 1922.[8]

So long as a natural cultural evolution and a creative rivalry with the past brought about the climate for a new kind of novel, fiction enjoyed its greatest achievements. But once the growing irrelevance of a divinity was articulated most dramatically by Nietzsche and Freud, once man's humiliated status was effectuated by Darwin's finishing off what Copernicus had begun, once the bourgeois foundations of society were shaken by Marx and exploded by world wars, with man's inhumanity to man taken to the last degree in the holocaust and the gulag, the institutions, manners, class structures, beliefs which the novel depended upon could no longer hold. The inexorable experimentation of form began to serve nothing deeper than itself. The forces which overthrew the great novels were beyond the power of anyone or thing to influence. And though social change was always in the cards, radical aggressive history dictated the terms and the tone. No longer could the books on the library shelves of Isak Dinesen's Cardinal turn their backs to the world for the sake of the story.[9]

The great novels – those written, with important exceptions, from the mid-eighteenth century to the mid-twentieth century – were never, not even *Tristram Shandy*, about themselves. It was evident to Fielding that although a good man within a small circle of friends is more deeply appreciated than he would be as a character in a book, nevertheless he can serve mankind in the latter capacity more extensively. And serve mankind Don Quixote did, writes Unamuno, "by giving the world cause to laugh at him."[10]

Don Antonio chastises the Knight of the White Moon, Sansón Carrasco, for the harm he has done the world "by seeking to deprive it of its most charming madman."[11] And Don Quixote himself feels he must quit his life of idleness with the duke "for he believed he was doing a great wrong in depriving the outside world of his presence…."[12] Such fame as he achieves – he hears of thousands of copies of his deeds published in many languages – must be for "my many valiant and Christian exploits." If a man has any other kind of fame than a good name, "his fate is worse than death."[13]

Georg Lukács recognizes that the "traces or lost meaning" we find in the classical novels sing "a song of comfort,"[14] allowing us, in a world no longer commensurate with our desires, to believe in the possibility of at least struggling towards a transcendental home. Though this literary tradition always respected suffering in contrast to Dostoevsky's anti-hero, the "underground man," who hasn't even "the slightest respect for [his own] suffering,"[15] these novels gave us comfort, as well, by placing us within the community of fellow sufferers. Reading great books, Robbie Turner thinks in Ian McEwan's *Atonement*, "can refine his sensibility towards the suffering of others" and make him a better doctor. Why not? Literature's business is also a physician's business – "Birth, death, and frailty in between" encompassing "the puniness and nobility of mankind."[16]

At Paddy Dignam's burial, Joyce's Bloom arms himself against the finality of death: "The ree the ra the ree the ra the roo. Lord, I mustn't lilt here," and uncle Toby whistles Lillabullero to ward off the bad news of the human condition. Yet reading about the deaths of Paul Dombey, Anna Karenina, Bazarov, Maggie and Tom Tulliver, Milly Theale and countless others, we feel strangely more alive, expansive, rich. Wonderfully so. "What draws the reader to the novel" writes Walter Benjamin, "is the hope of warming his shivering life with a death he reads about."[17] But in our rigorously unsentimental age, our faith in the healing power of novels fades and our authors are not interested in consoling. Quite the contrary.

For us, although we felt the great novels were not going to change the world, (part of the faint sense of melancholy we experienced while being lost in them), there did not seem to be such an abyss between literature and life. Lukács considered the epic to be a form in an age where man and his world were at one, and sees in the world of the nineteenth-century novel an inadequate breadth for the soul.[18] But the saving grace was that the great novels flourished when man was at least adequate to the world, resistant to it, worthy of it. Worthy in part because, as Auden reminds us, while we were reading these novels, they were reading us,[19] a better balance than Don Quixote's, who read the world, Michel Foucault observes, "in order to prove his books."[20]

The perversion of the relation between life and literature becomes evident in Dostoevsky's underground man, who avoids having to be a moral man by asserting that if they left "us alone without any books...we [should] at once get confused...we [should] not know what to hold onto, what to love and what to hate, what to respect and what to despise." A social gathering for him would be paltry and commonplace and, most distressing of all, unliterary.[21] In benign form, Parson Adams, whose emotions are very much alive, declares that "knowledge of men is only to be learnt from books,"[22] but Fielding, in the moral tradition, corrects this view by showing dramatically the dangers of choosing either living or reading to the exclusion of the other. In his philosophically bookish guise, the parson lectures Joseph about the need to cool his over-zealous love and passion for Fanny until life intrudes in the form of a false rumor that his own son has drowned, whereupon he goes passionately berserk.

"I love the old questions. Ah the old questions, the old answers, there's nothing like them," sighs Hamm when Beckett's Clov, in "End Game" complains to him that he has asked the same questions millions of times. But as Lionel Trilling theorizes, one day people got tired of a novelistic morality concerned with individuals "saving" themselves and "realizing" themselves."[23] What did literature have to do with life? Life "lives for itself, whether we like it or not,"[24] Etienne declares in Julio Cortázar's game novel, *Hopscotch*.

We might be able to detect a kind of desperation on the part of the traditional novelists who stood on the cusp of a new age. New forms of literature had to answer the temperament of the time, a time, Ortega suggests, when art might have taken on too heavy a burden in its moral seriousness and lost its lyric grace, restored, then, by a move to the circumference of life, as entertainment, diversion, sport, festivity, game.[25] Svevo's Zeno has given us, in another context, the motivation for the game novelist – to keep life, except for brief moments, from laughing louder than the author.[26]

All very well for Wordsworth to announce that the poet has the task of "creating the taste by which he is to be enjoyed,"[27] and making a go of it. But in the long run, culture has the better of the author more often than not. Sterne's novel rests comfortably in its moral assumptions, and appreciates a world "big with jest,"[28] as Tristram's father calls it, but a world which is a far cry from the tricky, strange, cold and uncongenial one of the modern novel of game, or the mean jests, for that matter, of Cervantes' Duke and Duchess. The kindly Don Antonio Moreno agrees with the proverb that "Jests that give pain are no jests at all." And Don Quixote tells the rowdies surrounding the Duke and Duchess to leave Sancho alone "for neither he nor I is fond of jests."[29] (Ishvar, in a rare modern masterpiece, Rohinton Mistry's *A Fine Balance*, agrees. When the sweaty cook roars over the stories of what happens to uncle and nephew, and declares they could produce a modern Mahabharat he replies "Please, bhai, no more adventures for us. Stories of suffering are no fun when we are the main characters.")[30]

But the uncharitable jests of Don Quixote which seem to victimize Sancho and his master are not the jests of the game novel precisely because they are carried out in the world of the New Testament, where the last can be first. And this comes about because "God's in his Heaven and sees all our tricks... ."[31] Farther on, the major-domo, surprised by Sancho's unlettered wisdom, recognizes such spiritual reversals: "Each day new things are seen in this world, jests are turned into earnest and jesters are mocked."[32] In the absence of this cultural sturdiness and belief, the novels of game punish the jester and the victim equally.

What's different about Sterne's spirit of games is expressed by Tristram's father, who knows that this world of jest "has wit in it, and instruction too, – if we can find it out."[33] And because the Shandean world is still legible and generous in its defining of character, meanness has no place in it. Gentle Uncle Toby's military strategies or Father's "thousand little skeptical notions of the comic kind," were mere whims with which Tristram's Father made merry "for half an hour or so, and having sharpened his wit upon them, dismissed them till another day."[34] But Joyce's Bloom is aware of "some impudent mocks which he however had borne with as being the fruits of that age upon which it is commonly charged that it knows not pity."[35] He would have much in common with Urbino in Gabriel García Márquez's novel *Love in the Time of Cholera*, who felt himself, in a "land of immortal pranksters," to be "in conflict with everything," his most "estimable virtues" provoking "the sly jokes of the younger ones."[36] Such modern ridicule is a far cry from the spiritual value of the ridicule Don Quixote faced as a kind of heroic holy fool.

It is no wonder, then, that so many of the serious authors on the modern scene chose novels of game, and hardly genial ones, at that. Of course there is much of our literature which does not fall under this rubric, but it seems to me the importance of the game novel is that it not only represents the temperament of the age; it signals the well-noted directions in which new "writing" is proceeding – absent or highly unreliable authors, plots that are simply tricks, abstract settings, unmotivated characters who serve a pattern and become one as well, and finally, the omnipotent "readers" who ascend the throne which the banished author has left, composing texts of their own.

Lukács' observation that "The immanence of meaning in life...had become a problem,"[37] true in his time, is even more true today, so that literature as Jonathan Franzen puts it, no longer possesses "the cultural authority"[38] it once did. It is not an accident that the titles of Ian McEwan's *Atonement* and Franzen's *Corrections* are morally freighted.

There are successes in this line, few though they be. In Jonathan Safran Foer's inventive *Everything Is Illuminated*, the holocaust has forced the grandfather to endure a choice grimly narrowed, the Jamesian *sine qua non* of a morally serious novel, as he must sacrifice his best friend for his own salvation. "Herschel was a good person and so was I."[39] But the holocaust cannot work for an author more than once. And it certainly does not work for W. G. Sebald, whose Vera wanders through post- holocaust Prague in *Austerlitz* mourning the death of her feelings. "Only in the books written in earlier times did she sometimes think she found some faint idea of what it might be like to be alive."[40]

Alive as a reader in the old Jamesian House of Fiction, a safe shelter in which the story, the author, the characters all have respect for one another, are responsible for one another, feel loyalty to one another. Even so anomalous a novel as *Tristram Shandy* shows the kind of tolerance that marks the very heart of this House. Its seemingly muddle-headed characters understand each other's hobby horses and allow ample room for their display. We find loyalty to the House taken to its final extreme in Ray Bradbury's modern fable *Fahrenheit 451*, as practiced by the remnant "book people" who become, for all intents and purposes, simply dust jackets for books they have memorized to save them from the pyre lit by the barbarians.

In the "metafiction"[41] of *Don Quixote*, a device authors from Laurence Sterne to Italo Calvino make use of, we find the knight of the mournful countenance and his squire conversing with their friend Sansón Carrasco about the author of their adventures, the corrections they might offer him and the hope that he will come up with a second part to the story, putting an end to spurious Don Quixotes and Sanchos. The danger with this self-conscious crossover of fiction and production, so common in the literature of game, is that it turns the novel, as Foucault puts it, into "the object of its own narrative."⁴²

But Cervantes does indeed deliver the great Part II! Don Quixote and Sancho Panza continue their adventures, and Cid Hamete Benengeli makes it clear that he is in control of the narrative (mostly), and the book remains the book. In the "metafiction" of today, however, the House of Fiction is no longer a sacred edifice to be preserved. In fact, it is barely standing at all. *If on a winter's night a traveler* addresses the reader concerning the novels he or she is reading. You can't get your bearings or recognize the characters, the setting, the plot. You can't recognize their integrity. "You begin to suspect that this is a different book, perhaps the real Polish novel *Outside the Town of Malbork*, whereas the beginning you have read could belong to yet another book, God only knows which."⁴³

Form as a Problem

We may welcome and lament at the same time the natural and unavoidable evolution of forms. Several cultural observers surmise that the accelerating pressure of inventiveness may, in our day, have caused the arts to hit a wall. It is fitting that *Don Quixote*, the matrix for the great line of eighteenth and nineteenth-century novels, should conduct what Claudio Guillen calls "an active dialogue of genres"[1] – the epic, picaresque, pastoral, chivalric, Bildungsroman, with diversionary tales and verse scattered throughout – all tumbling on the heels of one another in full confidence. Henry James may have called *War and Peace* a loose, baggy monster, but that monster was contained by the demands of its genre pushing against it. As this confidence wanes near the end of the great novelistic line, Joyce writes one of the most innovative novels in the English language, but has to do so by using all the old forms of literature perversely. His parodies demonstrate that he could no longer be comfortable about the moral resources available to him, but just look how, in one short exchange, he manages to make use of the fairy tale, the picaresque and the Bildungsroman: "Bloom: ...why did you leave your father's house? Stephen: To seek misfortune."[2] Joyce was hanging on to the tradition of the searching and learning paradigm in

A Portrait of the Artist as a Young Man and in *Ulysses*, where Stephen wanders through Dublin as a prelude to the great creative part he would play in the world.

This is the journey to which so many novelists who came after Joyce could no longer pay fealty, nor could Joyce himself. Such aimless restlessness carries with it the exhaustion of the work, as we see in Calvino's *If on a winter's night a traveler*, where one novel cannot reach the finish line before it falls into another. Morelli is the novelist in *Hopscotch* who relishes his task – the destruction of literary forms – by writing the antinovel. We should, he tells us, search for an opening in the closed order of the novel, "cut the roots of all systematic construction of characters and situations. Method: irony, ceaseless self-criticism, incongruity, imagination in the service of no one."[3] Morelli's creator relishes his task as well, as he sets up two different narratives, unfurling in every other line or asks the reader to go to Chapter 10 after he has read Chapter 50, and vice versa. It is telling that between the narratives of Cortázar's novel, whether they lie together on the page or, following the novel's metaphor, hop out of their cage altogether, there is no relation, none of that dialectical tension which marks the novels of the great tradition.

The picaresque, featuring the open road plain and simple, would seem to be the form least likely to engender dialectical tensions. But the road is seldom either plain or simple. Sancho tells his wife, and the innkeeper's wife as well, that it's a fine thing crossing mountains, woods, visiting castles, staying at inns. "Sometimes you look for one thing and you find another." Though in times of disillusion, it was not fun for Sancho to trail after his master "along roads that lead nowhere and highways and byways that don't deserve the name…,"[4] this suited Tristram Shandy just fine for his metaphorical picaresque. On his narrative journey, traveling straightway would be "morally speaking, impossible: For, if [the author] is a man of the least spirit he will have fifty deviations from a straight line to make with this or that party as he goes along, which he can no ways avoid." Sterne believes deeply that digressions are "the life, the soul of reading."[5]

The roads which the knight and his squire travel do not just try the body; they set up a dialectic by being, as well, what D. H. Lawrence calls "the great home of the Souls."⁶ And if one views the river in *Huckleberry Finn* as a road, it, too, is a home of the Souls; it is T. S. Eliot's "strong brown god," a god, Trilling reminds us, which appears "to embody a great moral idea,"⁷ so that Mark Twain has written a book which, on the one hand, is a quintessential picaresque and on the other, a kind of Bildungsroman in which a moral and spiritual education unfolds.

This river/god is used to powerful effect in García Márquez' *Love in the Time of Cholera* as well. "The trouble is that without river navigation there is no love,"⁸ Ariza's uncle tells his nephew, and he is right, for it is on the river that the two old lovers find their unique consummation. But since the river is a god, their love takes on a kind of spiritual dimension, which we always hope for in our reading. Ariza's letters to Fermina differed from those he had written in his youth. "They were, rather, the words of a man who...was inspired by the Holy Spirit." And he counted on his meditations to teach her "to think of love as a state of grace...."⁹

Since the great novelistic genres encompassed the necessary unmediated dialectics in the prevalent Christian cultural tradition, opposing perspectives of history and heaven were there for the asking, a tradition which colored, as well, the distinctions of class, the solidity of institutions, the intensity of place, the extension of time.

While instructing Sancho how to be a governor, the Don reminds him "that...mercy shines brighter in our eyes than does that of justice."¹⁰ But such empathy means little when it is expressed exclusively in terms of class. Don Quixote gives a Pauline explanation to Sancho that if the head suffers all other members suffer. "Being your master and lord, I am your head, and you, being my servant, are a part of me and so it is that the evil which affects me must likewise affect you and your pain must be my own," a pain he does not always succeed in sharing, witness the squire's bruising in a blanket tossing. You should know, Sancho, "that it is characteristic of noble and generous hearts to pay no attention to trifles."¹¹

Once class is established, however, Cervantes can move to the spiritual counterforce. The Don invites his squire to sit with him around the fire with the goatherds and drink from the same cup, "for of knight-errantry one may say the same as of love: that it makes all things equal and resembles on earth a fleeting moment of the heavenly scene; whosoever humbleth himself, him God will exalt. In that golden age, that blessed era, all things were held in common and no one judged or was judged."[12]

The reversal value of class in the determination of virtue and vice is a pervasive educative quality of the great novels. Fielding is comfortable describing "not men but manners; not an individual but a species." His Sir Thomas "was too apt to estimate men merely by dress, or fortune; and my lady…with a town education, …never spoke of any of her country neighbors by any other appellation than that of the Brutes."[13]

But, in making sexual demands of Joseph, Lady Booby is caught off guard by his purity: "I can't see why [the lady's] having no virtue should be a reason against my having any; or why, because I am a man, or because I am poor, my virtue must be subservient to her pleasures…."[14]

Since Joseph was only a poor foot passenger, the surgeon would not attend him at the inn, and when the Master of the Inn wishes to give Joseph his shirt, his wife objects, for "common charity teaches us to provide for ourselves, and our families; and I and mine won't be ruined by your charity, I assure you."[15] But the humble postilion lad had already given Joseph his coat when all the upper-class travelers in the carriage refuse to give him theirs. Such examples of the uncharitable haves and the charitable have-nots in the traditional novels abound. It is easy enough to run through Balzac and Austen and Dickens, Zola and Trollope for the workings of morality through class.

Within the solid social structure of these novels, the family unit is often the crucible of moral depth. The formation of family has its origin for Sancho Panza at the "dinner table." When his master sits down to eat with the goatherds, he wants Sancho to sit by his side and eat from his plate and drink what he drinks, for knight-errantry makes all things equal. Sancho prefers to eat standing up but Don Quixote insists. "And, laying hold of his squire's arm, he compelled him to take a seat beside him."[16] That gesture seals a bond which becomes so strong, class is erased both in words and in rhetoric; at a later time, Don Quixote borrows a proverb from Sancho: "Not with whom you are bred, but with whom you are fed."[17]

Don Quixote is quite aware of breaches in the social hierarchy. The very fact that Sancho talks incessantly to him demonstrates that the servant does not have enough respect and the master does not make himself more respected. But such interchanges cause Sancho to realize the company of his master gave him more pleasure than "the governorship of all the islands in the world."[18] Though the squire, locked into cultural aphorisms, is more than a little credulous, he can surely be seen as a forerunner (and there were others before him) of the clever and insolent servant so evident in Jacques, who crosses over from tension to friendship with the master. Sancho's leave-taking from the Don as he goes off to his island brings forth tears of affection. These are family sentiments in the way of Trim and uncle Toby, where the hearts of both the master and the man "were alike subject to sudden overflowings."[19]

It is the intense presence of family, in fact, which keeps Tristram Shandy in the novelistic tradition. Tristram's Father, with a rash temperament, denigrates uncle Toby's military strategic obsessions. But once he sees the good nature shining on Toby's countenance, he asks for forgiveness. "'My dear, dear brother', answer'd my uncle Toby...'you are heartily welcome, had it been ten times as much....'" "...tis ungenerous, replied my father, to hurt any man; – a brother worse; – but to hurt a brother of such gentle manners...tis base....'."[20]

We can expand the family concept through the metaphor of "infection" which runs through Cervantes' novel and has its way of uniting the family of man. At one time or another, characters, including Sancho, seem to be as mad as Don Quixote whose speech has been infected, in turn, by Sancho's proverbs. Even authorial duties become infectious, shared by the reliable and the unreliable, by the high-born in shepherd's clothing and the plagiarists. Finally, the barriers of species are crossed. Rocinante and Sancho's gray are inseparable, so much, in fact, that their friendship alone becomes legend, "handed down from father to son." And the human family embraces the animal world as well, for, as Cid Hamete observes, "he seldom saw Sancho Panza without the ass or the ass without Sancho Panza, such was the friendship and loyalty that existed between them."[21]

The dialectic within the traditional genres between the family of men and the family of man must embrace relationships as the family itself becomes more tenuous, as society becomes more problematic. If Jim's family is to be destroyed by society's edicts, he must form a kind of primitive community with Huck as exiles on the river. It is the ocean which, in the end, makes the crew of Conrad's Narcissus a band of brothers. "Haven't we, together and upon the immortal sea, wrung out a meaning from our sinful lives?" Bloom, so desperate to find company in the Dublin pub's rejecting crowd, whips himself into a frenzied recital of belonging – "Mendelssohn was a jew and Karl Marx and Mercadante and Spinoza. And the Saviour was a Jew and his father was a Jew. Your God...."[22] And he manages to form a kind of symbolic father-son bond with Stephen, of different temperament and background but like him, a wanderer in the city, the city that possesses them despite their estrangement.

Stephen fails in his wishes to "merge his life in the common tide of other lives,"[23] causing his doubts and scruples to grow, his soul to feel that spiritual dryness of the underground man, who, as a precursor, had given up his desire to merge long ago. In the modern, permanent exile, we come finally to the full realization that "the ways leading to the transcendental home have become impassable."[24]

For the modern novel, problems of interrelational communication in an unpossessed world grow ever more severe. Whereas Turgenev can write a deep novel about the unbridgeable gap between generations, Calvino's Palomar lives in an age "when young people's impatience with the old and old people's impatience with the young have reached their peak... The difficulty lies in the fact that between us and them there is an unbridgeable gap. Something has happened between our generation and theirs, a continuity of experience has been broken: we no longer have any common reference points."[25]

In Gaddis' *JR* there are frantic attempts to hook up, to mend broken homes, to join child with parent, to claim inheritances and familial identity, far beyond any world of exile the self-described foster child Stephen Dedalus lived in. The novel gives us lawyers and legal complications, all the good stuff of the classic stories, but no community; only intense loneliness. And this is because if, like Mr. Palomar, characters do not "live in harmony with the world,"[26] they have a difficult time establishing relations.

It is evident that the sense of exile must push against a sense of place; the very words "exile" or "return" tell us that there is a place. D. H. Lawrence knew that the road was the home of the soul but he knew, as well, that "the spirit of place is a great reality."[27] Deep moral concerns, strong stories, depended upon that England or France or Russia whose social world and its ways were testing places for character growth. To narrow Wallace Stevens' definition in *The Necessary Angel*, it is the moral imagination which emerges from the mind pressing against reality.

García Màrquez's Fermina Daza has stayed in place with her husband, surrounded by a varied, full-bodied and voiced community who come knocking on her door – the milkman, the fishwife, fruit and vegetable sellers, beggars, girls with lottery tickets, sisters of charity, the knife grinder with ready gossip, the man who buys bottles, old gold, newspapers, fake gypsies reading fortune in cards, on palms, in coffee grounds or washbasin water. In their singularities, this crowd is a far cry from those who people the "maximalist" novels, with all their wild detail and behavior – clowns, rock bands, shysters, criminals, con men, wanderers, bums, drug addicts, drunks, kinky partners. The salient point about this profusion is that they do not belong to a community but are deracinated in such a way that unlike the wanderers in the picaresque genre, they would not be pilgrims of the soul.

Ironically, it is the very social thickness of the world García Márquez has created which allows him to throw against that solidity characters free of all earthly entanglements. Once Florentino Ariza, who was seen by his mistresses as a casual man, reunites with Fermina, he makes of her a woman dreaming of "mad voyages, free of trunks, free of social commitments: voyages of love."[28]

Anchises and then Aeneas carry their *lares* and *penates* with them throughout their travels until the hero reaches his new home, as Ulysses reached his old one. But the modern exile journeys over the earth without place or gods. In Calvino's *Invisible Cities*, the *lares* and *penates* of the City of Leandra have become a joke. And Sebald's Austerlitz recalls wandering through the queen of cities, "the empty Sunday streets of

Paris taking hundreds of Banlieu-photographs, as I called them, pictures which in their very emptiness, as I realized only later, reflected my orphaned frame of mind."[29]

Wandering aimlessly, as well, is the protagonist in Cortázar's *Hopscotch*, without purpose or anchor, regretting the only love of his life, La Maga, whom he left in Paris and who disappears mysteriously. Horacio, has the "motives of a destroyer of compasses," with "nothing in mind."[30] He has the longing necessary for a dialectical pattern but he has nothing working against it, as Conrad's characters, for instance, have so effectively. "If the novel should really disappear," Kundera observes, "it will do so not because it has exhausted its powers but because it exists in a world grown alien to it."[31] If exile means that there was once a place, we might rightly call the contemporary novels exiles par excellence, for it is the indispensable sense of place that is missing.

Isak Dinesen's Cardinal tells us that where there is the story, the characters will come.[32] But the story has to have a place to which the characters can come. And so divorced from the sense of place is the modern world that artifice must be used to lure Madame Pace into "Six characters in search of an author" by building a set that replicates her environment outside the play as it is described by the characters.

Of course Henry James was already complaining of emptiness in America, obliging him to go to Europe for his customs, institutions, history, and giving him as well his oppositional motif of the old world and the new. Still, there was enough social resistance to make the quintessential American Huck think hard before his conscience took over. As Theodor Adorno puts it, "The novel" has long had "as its true subject matter the conflict between living human beings and rigidified conditions,"[33] but in recent years, we count chiefly on the British mysteries called "cozies," already dated, with their small vicarage towns, structured societies, church, state, home, school, professions, widows and spinsters, doctors, clergy, for a sense of place, a weak reminder of that old Dickensian world of London's mews, prisons, lanes, clerks and pubs, courts of chancery and Lincoln Inn chambers.

In a disintegrating world, Henry James finds contrasting continents, Lawrence his coal mining towns thick with class structure, Conrad his naval microcosms, Hardy his Wessex, and Kafka, his dreamlike and absurdist Prague and Amerika. So it is not surprising that the few really deep genre novels written in the latter half of the twentieth century and early twenty-first centuries are the ones that manage to find worlds with stratification – V. S. Naipaul's *A House for Mister Biswas*, Rohinton Mistry's *A Fine Balance*, García Márquez' *Love in the Time of Cholera*, regional novels by Faulkner and Flannery O'Connor – because they must deal with caste, class, history, institutions, a sense of place, all the weight the world throws against their characters.

As Bloom wanders through Dublin, his sense of place and time produces dynamic oppositions to his universal imagination. "And I belong to a race that is hated and persecuted. Also now. This very moment. This very instant. ...I'm talking about injustice... Force, hatred, history, all that... That's not life for men and women, insult and hatred. And everybody knows that it's the very opposite of that that is really life.

 - What? Says Alf.

 - Love, says Bloom, I mean the opposite of hatred...." And after he leaves, the citizen calls him "A new apostle to the gentiles... Universal love."[34]

It is the sense of his city that gives Bloom a way to move to universals of birth and death by broadening particular news bits of Dublin. Take the section called "Hades". Bloom thinks of his personal losses – the suicide of his father, the untimely death of his son Rudy, even the classical Athos, his father's dog pining away. Dignam's funeral gives way to three hundred kicking the bucket, three hundred being born, a cityful passing away, another cityful coming only to pass away as well. And finally to "funerals all over the world everywhere every minute. Shovelling them under by the cartload doublequick. Thousands every hour. Too many in the world."[35] (As Mina Purefoy gives birth and Dignam is buried, keep in mind how Robbie Turner of *Atonement* thinks literature enhances his medical calling: "Birth, death, and frailty in between. Rise and fall.")

García Márquez' novels manage to establish a sense of place even in defiance of time and history. When Dr. Juvenal Urbino of *Love in the Time of Cholera* returns from Paris, the sight of his "sleepy provincial capital" and its dilapidated structures, the city of the Viceroy, the city of his youth where "old families sank into their ruined palaces in silence" depresses him. But the place draws the character as potently as the story does, when he realizes "this was his world...the sad, oppressive world that God had provided for him, and he was responsible to it."[36] Urbino possesses his place as it possesses him while Calvino's traveler wanders through invisible and unpossessed cities of the imagination.[37]

Calvino's old Marco Polo of *Invisible Cities* leafs through the Great Khan's atlas which can describe "the form of cities that do not yet have a form or a name."[38] But those places we have named are all the same. When you arrive in the Trude airport, it looks like the airport you took off from. "You can resume your flight whenever you like...but you will arrive at another Trude, absolutely the same, detail by detail. The world is covered by a sole Trude which does not begin and does not end. Only the name of the airport changes."[39] (Will "the end of all our exploring" be, after all, "to arrive where we started" and never know the place for the first time?)[40] The author takes the loss of place to its extreme in *If on a winter's night a traveler.* "The city outside there has no name yet, we don't know if it will remain outside the novel or whether the whole story will be contained within its inky blackness."[41]

For all the ghostliness of cities, there could still be the possibility of polarities if there would be a place called country, where relationships and customs offered a contrast, as these virtues once clashed with the corruption and loneliness of the cities in the traditional novels. Joseph Andrews writes to Pamela: "London is a bad place and there is so little good fellowship, that the next-door neighbors don't know one another."[42] Sancho Panza, by contrast, has known Don Quixote since birth and comes from the same town.

Manzoni, who lived in the country and thought cities the saddest of places, plays beautifully with this opposition in *I Promessi Sposi*. And Bloom dreams, as he wanders through Dublin's streets, of a country bungalow. But as in Balzac, the dichotomy can break both ways, so that leaving the small country world of birth, close families and limitations, the protagonist meets the broadening and deepening of relationships and experience, the coming of age in the wider world, a world as wide as the young protagonist in *A Portrait of the Artist as a Young Man* imagines when he signs the flyleaf of his geography book Stephen Dedalus, Class of Elements, Clongowes Wood College, Sallins, County Kildare, Ireland, Europe, The World, The Universe.[43]

The sense of time, as important as place in the great novels, controlled the linear narrative in both picaresque novels and the Bildungsroman, with enough freedom to utilize flashbacks, digressive and competing stories, utopian or dire projections. (The segment of time, of course, needn't be confined so long as it is somewhat resolved. Zola's and Balzac's and Joyce's characters sometimes march off into the next book.)

Even a novel like *Tristram Shandy*, which would seem to scorn the periodicity of time and plot, depends upon our idea of a structured sequential narrative to resist and play with. Since the novel appears in the tradition of time narrative novels, its experiments with time only confirm our anchor by its absence. (We might note that the very conception of Tristram is compromised from the beginning by a question about the winding of the grandfather clock.)

García Márquez has figured out how, with his magical realism, he can make even a loss of time as palpable an entity as place. In *One Hundred Years of Solitude*, Ursula realizes, through repetitive names, generations, wars, that time doesn't pass, but turns in a circle. Macondo is visited by history in the making with the advent of the train and other "amenities," only to sink, in the end, back into timeless decay.

Or, its very petrification gives it weight. Urbino's city stands "unchanging on the edge of time: the same burning dry city of his nocturnal terrors...where nothing had happened for four centuries, except a slow aging among withered laurels and putrefying swamps."[44] And the author changes the terms of "progressive" by successfully producing a great novel which opposes the segment of fifty-three years, seven months, and eleven days and nights of unfulfilled love against another world of "forever" which sets Ariza and Fermina free from time's grip altogether.

If on a Winter's Night a Traveler, by contrast, written in the modern void, not only shatters the dimension of time, (which could be said as well of *Tristram Shandy*), but eliminates character, place, the novel itself. The narrator tells us, as we are about to read, that "we cannot love or think except in fragments of time each of which goes off along its own trajectory and immediately disappears. We can rediscover the continuity of time" and, we might add, place, "only in the novels of that period when time no longer seemed stopped and did not yet seem to have exploded, a period that lasted no more than a hundred years,"[45] a period, we note, of great storytelling.

Trilling imagines students might wish, in reading Jane Austen, "to transcend our sad contemporary existence, that, from the world of our present weariness and desiccation, they might reach back to a world which, as it appears to the mind's eye, is so much more abundantly provided with trees than with people, a world in whose green shade life for a moment might be a green thought."[46] But, as we know, with Kundera, we no longer have the possibility of that green life. "It's some time now since the river, the nightingale, the paths through the fields have disappeared from man's mind. No one needs them now. When nature disappears from the planet tomorrow, who will notice?"[47]

We are beyond the axed trees of "The Cherry Orchard," beyond those of Ombrosa in which Calvino's Baron had lived. Ombrosa no longer exists. "Looking at the empty sky, I ask myself if it ever did really exist" writes the Baron's brother at the end of the story. And at the end of their story, Fermina and Ariza sail into their eternal love past ravaged forests and animals, with corpses floating down the river, dynamited fish, alligators that had eaten the last butterfly and the maternal manatees which were gone. The parrots, the monkeys, the villages were gone; everything was gone.

It seems churlish to blame later authors for their loss of power, given their need to work up their stories in the midst of unstructured, despoiled and ever fluid societies, the absence of belief and institutions in all forms, the empty or interchangeable settings, the ravages of an overwhelming and unimaginable history in a universe that has selected its own plots and has forgone a stable morality, the inexorable globalization, terrorism, instant communication, transportation, trade, acceleration, distraction, restlessness, MTV, the separation of families and communities, the insatiable need for an incessant narrative of news and documentaries, but that is their burden.

The self answers the missing structures with its own reductions: Mr. Palomar, "a nervous man who lives in a frenzied and congested world...tends to reduce his relations with the outside world; and, to defend himself against the general neurasthenia, he tries to keep his sensations under control insofar as possible."[48] Into Palomar's flat world, Calvino has moved from his densely populated *The Baron in the Trees*, where his protagonist, who lives in the trees, still manages to work his sweeping perspectives dramatically to earn the inscription on the family tomb – "Cosimo Piovasco di Rondo – Lived in trees – Always loved earth – Went into sky". But by the time we get to his *Invisible Cities*, perspectives become games of the mind, where infernal cities are architectural masterpieces and heavenly cities are "a-flutter with potato peels, broken umbrellas, old socks, candy wrappings, paved with tram tickets, fingernail-cuttings and pared calluses, eggshells".[49]

Morality as a Problem

If the end of the Victorian age put a stop to the lesser novels of memorized morality[1], the novel of game finished off the great novels of moral imagination which accommodated moral oppositions clashing under the auspices and within expectations of a solid social framework. In the novel of game, morality is irrelevant, whereas the play in *Rameau's Nephew* is not. Diderot (like Mandeville) would seem to free vice and virtue from the prison of the absolute in good enlightenment style by playing an appearance and reality game with them; what we call vice seems more like virtue and virtue vice.[2] But we should keep in mind that Sterne and Diderot felt free to play with the moral canon precisely because they could count on its presence.

Authors who knew, as Nietzsche contends the English, and George Eliot in particular, did not, that morality had become a problem,[3] were charged with finding ways that would take them back to the old questions and answers. But it was tough sledding. In Trollope, the large moral conversions of the Victorians dribble away into scruples. And it is chiefly linguistic invention, "agenbite of inwit,"[4] which helps Joyce hang on to the morality of guilt in an age which is making it meaningless.

Kafka and Beckett are equally ingenious as they manage to cling to the old oppositions in an absurd world by turning crime and punishment on their heads. With Raskolnikov, Kundera points out, we have an offense seeking a punishment, in Kafka, a punishment seeking an offence.[5] Though the wily Zeno longs to recapture the inexpressible delight "of being able to live again one day of innocence and inexperience," he understands that the world has lost its dialectical clarity. "Life is "neither good nor bad, it is original."[6]

Ringing a dandy change on the good and evil of Jekyll and Hyde, Calvino, in *The Cloven Viscount*, splits one Viscount into two halves which carry the moral burden of good and evil cunningly but deeply. (And a far cry from the simplistic Manichean forms of today's comics, graphic novels, pulp fiction, sci fi, film fantasies, multi-universes, computer games.) Everything in the human and natural world of Calvino's story was split. "So man moved against himself, both hands armed with swords."[7]

In his later works, however, good and evil, guilt and innocence become ridiculous. Looking at the sky with a telescope, the nameless "he" of *Cosmicomiche* notices a sign hanging from a galaxy a hundred million light-years away, upon which is written, I SAW YOU. But the moment when "they" had observed him must date back 200 million years. It certainly doesn't sound as if the nameless "they" had observed a good deed, which means "he" should feel guilty about something he must have done or hadn't done centuries ago. Were they talking about a time he picked his nose? Only if the galaxies disappear forever could he have peace.[8] But we can cop a smile.

A central dialectic of all novels, as so many critics have observed, is that of appearance and reality in a multitude of variations, but in the novels of the great flowering it serves as a moral marker for seeing clearly and acting well. *Don Quixote* features the conflict between what the world is and what the world ought to be, but the droll inability of the Don to see clearly compromises the moral necessity of acting well. While he hears horses, trumpets, drums, Sancho sees only sheep. But as there are times Sancho falls under the spell of enchantment, so there are times when the deluded Don Quixote pays homage to reality in his contrary way. "It may be that, inasmuch as you (Don Fernando, the curate, the barber, Cardenio) have not been dubbed knights as I have been, your Worships will not be subject to the enchantments of this place and, accordingly, your judgment being unimpaired, will be able to form an impression of things in this castle as they really and truly are and not as they appear to me to be."[9]

Only when appearance can no longer be a worthy opponent to reality must we be prepared for Don Quixote to leave the book. "They took up their journey once more, being in haste to reach an inn which they could see... I say inn, for the reason that this was what Don Quixote called it, contrary to his usual custom of calling all inns castles."[10]

As we move into the Bildungsroman, however, seeing well does not banish the protagonists from the book but, on the contrary, renders them stronger. Jarndyce's realization of how the Neckett children in the East End of London really live by seeing them with his own eyes represents one of the key passages of *Bleak House*: "Look at this! For God's sake, look at this!"[11] And the scales fall off the eyes of James' Isabel Archer when she sits in front of the fire and works out the drama of deceptive appearance which has victimized her.

Even so inventive and mischievous a storyteller as Calvino uses illusion and disillusion, the romance and the real, to fine effect in his earlier writings. At the end of *The Cloven Viscount*, the boy, who has fallen under the spell of the fanciful Doctor Trelawney, watches the ship carry him away. "Take me with you" he shouts but it is too late: "...already the ships were vanishing over the horizon and I was left behind, in this world of ours full of responsibilities and will-o'-the-wisps."[12]

But what has happened to the conflict between appearance and reality with Mr. Palomar, who banishes appearance in order to see clearly from his terrace, a good observation post. "Things being as they are, then, Mr. Palomar has decided to confine himself to watching, to establishing down to the slightest detail what little he sees, sticking to the immediate ideas that what he sees suggests."[13] Here, seeing clearly does not lead into the expansion of the soul nor even to any form of social discourse.

The calamitous results are illuminated in Nabokov's *The Defense*, where the chess playing Luzhin sees patterns everywhere but people nowhere, and Sebald's Austerlitz, not unlike Luzhin, imagines "the black and white diamond pattern of the stone slabs beneath my feet were the board on which the endgame would be played."[14]

In a preface, Richard Rorty discusses the central opposition he finds in the wonderfully clever and subtle game novel *Pale Fire*,[15] between the beauty we see in Kimbote's fable and the pity we feel for Shade's daughter (the old dialectic of aesthetics and morality) as one which gives the book its tension and gravity. Precisely because we are so enchanted with Kimbote's story, we forget about Hazel Shade's tragedy, and the pity becomes more poignant when we return to it. But we could argue that the scale tips too far in one direction. Nabokov's use of appearance and its concomitant deceptions actually limits the moral capacity of the novel. The author tricks the mad narrator-protagonist, and often the lazy reader, more for the sheer creative joy of it than for a weightier purpose. Kimbote never really learns to see, but his obtuseness can hardly be blamed for the death of Shade.

One of the reasons García Márquez' *Love in the Time of Cholera* is so powerful, however magical its realism, is that it plays a surprising variation on illusion and disillusion twice during the novel. This opposition no longer holds its customary position at the end, but shows up at the beginning. Fermina Daza has dealt with the disappointment in her marriage – "nothing in this world was more difficult than love" – but through victories over adversity, she sees the beauty of her thirty-year relationship with her husband, who confesses his ardent love to her in his dying. They have come out "on the other shore."[16]

Now, has disillusion ever been handled more skillfully than the moment when, as a widow, Fermina Daza sees her first love again and feels nothing? Yet from that disillusion, she falls under the spell of Ariza's illusion – the magical realism of his unceasing love through time – and this acceptance overcomes the decay of the body. Ariza, anything but a "moral" man, adores a woman "who longed for no other happiness but death," yet despite his bald head, his false teeth, his odd dress, his limp, he makes her believe they had "leapt over the arduous calvary of conjugal life and gone straight to the heart of love."[17] Within the magical realism genre itself lies the creative dialectic for the author, who learned from the stories of Kafka and his grandmother how to recount "the wildest things with a completely natural tone of voice" and to believe in them.[18] In this he was not much removed from Don Quixote.

We can trace the growth of the morally serious novel easily enough, and its subsequent evolution into novels of game, but then there is always the problem of *Tristram Shandy*. Taking into account the fact that Sterne was writing in the temper of the times, the eighteenth century as the age of play, we still want to acknowledge its position in the line of the great novels. Yorick's Sermon about inner conscience is, in its way, serious enough, but that is hardly what we mean by the moral imagination. Though we can never regret, as Kundera does, the deviation into the "morally serious" nineteenth-century novel which literature took after *Tristram Shandy* and Diderot's homage to Sterne in *Jacques le fataliste*, both of which had so many of the characteristics of game novels, we too wonder why.[19]

Richard Lanham asks the primary question for us. What kind of morality is possible in a Shandean world, in a book which pokes fun at seriousness?[20] We remember how Tristram assured us, tongue in cheek, that for a man of spirit, going straightway would be "morally speaking," impossible.[21] He describes his father as "a good natural philosopher, -------yet he was something of a moral philosopher too...", which is followed by a dilemma over what to do with his broken pipe.[22] But it seems sensible and by no means forced, to read Sterne's book not only as a form breaker and a precursor of the game novel, but as an adherent, in its way, through its playfulness and its family ties, of the strain of moral seriousness which characterizes the traditional novel. The author effectively makes use of a moral vocabulary while at the same time teasing it, which is one reason the Victorians turned thumbs down on this work.

The novel as game, however, the appropriate form for our time, exists outside of culture, obsessed with contrivances and self-referentiality. When writers turn to absurdist literature to compensate for the world's refusal to recognize or allow their more expansive longings, we can hardly accuse them, as Jacques Barzun does, of a failure of nerve.[23] We see the shrinkage of the canvas. Mr. Palomar reasons that "It is only after you have come to know the surface of things...you can venture to seek what is underneath," but he never arrives at that point for "the surface of things is inexhaustible."[24] This is the world of Alain Robbe-Grillet, a "flat and discontinuous universe where each thing refers only to itself."[25] Whether the novel of game is located entirely in fantasy or obsessively in realism, there is no dialectical tension.

In Calvino's *Cosmicomiche*, the unmanageable wide spaces from earth to heaven do not offer meaningful perspectives; the numbers flashing through endless generations and space are just as likely to be betting formulae, the signs simply unrelated. Have we come, again, through the Internet, into pre-historic times when "In the universe...there was no longer a container and a thing contained, but only a general thickness of signs superimposed and coagulated, occupying the whole volume of space ...."? The game novel thrives in a world where we have "no longer any way to establish a point of reference...."[26]

A universe where there is no longer a container or a thing contained is represented most directly by the "maximalist" novel, abetted by the computer's logorrhea, featuring gobs of unselected, undigested facts. The author's aesthetic distance, so nurtured in Henry James, no longer exists. Oscar Wilde saw this coming. "The ancient historians gave us delightful fiction in the form of fact; the modern novelist presents us with dull facts under the guise of fiction,"[27] or, in the more entertaining mode, some modern novelists, as John Bayley frames it, "involuntarily underline the significance of fact even while modishly engaged in calling it in question."[28] To compensate for the loss of characters and manners, armies of wild eccentrics prance through fantastic scenarios, to compensate for loss of plot, unmotivated and unimaginable situations, to make up for the loss of place, gorgeous sentences that go nowhere. The more these novels are stuffed, the thinner the story feels so that maximalism, in the long run, becomes a form of minimalism

In Mr. Palomar, we find a perfect combination of the two. Palomar decides that he will set himself to describing every instant of his life and until he has described them all he will no longer think of being dead. At that moment he dies – dies because he is no longer a part of the world.[29]

It is impossible for The House of Fiction to hold such frustration. The absurdity of Pirandello's drama "Six characters in search of an author" reflects what is happening in the novels, as characters become authors and audience, spilling across the stage into real life. The genre falls apart. *If on a winter's night a traveler* has no plot, characters, author, sense of place, duration of time, narrative. Finally the book itself, dissolves before our eyes. Ian McEwan's Briony, in *Atonement*, understands what is happening: "The age of clear answers was over." And as an author, herself, she knows what this means. Finished "was the age of characters and plots,"[30] finished as well, the unassailable authority of the author. Post-modern critics have tirelessly and tiresomely dismembered the whole crew. But it is important to note that this decomposition began in a betrayal of the very story which held them all together.

The Truth of the Story

Dinesen's Cardinal becomes blasphemous when he declares "In the beginning was the story," for this can only mean that the creation of the heaven and the earth had to come into being only after the "divine art" of its telling.[1] And divine art it is. "There is no boon in life more sweet" for Odysseus "than when a summer joy holds all the realm, / and banqueters sit listening to a harper / in a great hall...."[2] And in the great hall of *Beowulf*, "carrier[s] of stories" play on the "timbered harp," and the past wells up in the "wintry heart" of an old veteran.[3]

Which does not mean the story will stay put. Even Don Quixote understands in a moment of lucidity. "So, this that appears to you as a barber's basin," he tells Sancho, "is for me Mambrino's helmet and something else again to another person...."[4] Furthermore, the knight lives in a story which contains Chinese boxes of other stories, other narrators; even his own narrative has been plagiarized. And still the story holds. Once the packsaddle becomes a caparison and the basin Mambrino's helmet, they remain so until the Day of Judgment. Once the broken-down nag and the peasant girl become Rocinante and Dulcinea, once Sancho on his gray and Don Quixote on his nag ride out to their adventures, they become eternal embodiments and protectors of the story.

Is it not strange that Don Quixote should believe Dorotea's tale, asks the curate. "It is indeed," answers Cardenio, "so rare and unheard of a thing that if anyone desired to invent and fabricate it, in the form of fiction, I do not know if there would be any mind that would be equal to the task."[5] When writers like Cervantes, Diderot, Fielding speak of their true histories rather than their stories, when their characters swear that their story is truer than another, as Cervantes' Arcadian shepherds and shepherdesses do, we understand the game they are playing because we believe in the truth of stories.

In his beginning pages, Cervantes tells us he is interested more in the truth of the story than in the facts. The difference of opinion concerning Don Quixote's real name "means very little so far as our story is concerned, providing that in the telling of it we do not depart one iota from the truth." The story, in the form of art, should keep us from dying of the truth, according to Nietzsche, and it was that truth, not the truth of the story, that killed Don Quixote.

He who has been a protector of his stories finally, upon his death bed, turns on them by confessing he had invented the tale of the Cave of Montesinos because it seemed to him to fit well with those adventures he had read of in storybooks. The jig is up, but not for his book. The "true" is more powerful than the "real."

Jacques' author insists he is writing history. "It is quite obvious that I am not writing a novel since I am neglecting those things which a novelist would not fail to use. The person who takes what I write for the truth might perhaps be less wrong than the person who takes it for a fiction."[6] But for all his tricks and disclaimers, the important thing to note is that Diderot's narrator keeps his story and his characters safe from authorial incursions. "You are going to believe that this little army [in the inn] will fall upon Jacques and his master, that there will be a bloody fight, blows with sticks, and pistol shots and if I wanted to, I could make all these things happen, but then it would be goodbye to the truth of the story and goodbye to the story of Jacques's love."[7]

In novels like *Tristram Shandy* and *Jacques le fataliste*, the stories the characters tell sometimes go astray. "Bohemia! Said my uncle Toby... What became of that story, Trim? – "We lost it, an' please your honour, somehow betwixst us."[8] And Jacques loses his stories to persistent interruptions as well. But Toby and Trim and Father and Jacques and his master and their stories, however interrupted and incomplete, never change because they live safely in the House of Fiction.

The truth of the story mattered to Calvino early in his career, confirmed by the *Baron in the Trees* who tells tales of his adventures and makes up new ones for the folk of Ombrosa, stories which, "originally true, became, as he told them, invented, and from invented, true."[9] (The anecdotes of Svevo's Zeno "began to be true from the moment when it would have been impossible for me to tell a story differently."[10] And so persuasive is the truth of his story, his wife tells him long afterwards, that though none of her family believed his stories, she liked them better for their invention, because they seemed to belong more to Zeno than if they had actually happened to him).

But in Calvino's later work, the stories not only can be told in any version desired; in fact, they don't have to be told at all. Ludmilla's sister Lotaria in *If on a winter's night a traveler*, a character of dizzying identifications, presses the wrong key and erases the entire text of a book, whereupon a new story begins.[11]

Just as the cities Marco Polo describes in *Invisible Cities* go in every direction, up into the air and underground, so too do Calvino's tales. One of the many narrators in *If on a winter's night a traveler* knows he is "producing too many stories at once because what I want is for you to feel, around the story, a saturation of other stories that I could tell and maybe will tell or who knows may already have told...a space full of stories...where you can move in all directions as in space, always finding stories that cannot be told until other stories are told first etc."[12]

The story must protect itself, as Sterne reminds us in his dedication. (We can find an illustration of how such protection can work against an incursion in a modern work like *Everything Is Illuminated*. The character Alex writes to the character Jonathan, who is also the author: "I do not think that there are any limits to how excellent we could make life seem,"[13] but the final irony of this desire lies in the secrets of the holocaust which the story uncovers.) The truth in the story supports the truth of the story. And the story must protect its characters as well. Now when the story is faithful to the characters, the characters are faithful to the story. Don

Quixote puts his reputation on the line for the truth of the story when he asks the skeptical merchants to swear, without seeing her, that Dulcinea is the most beautiful woman in the world. "If I were to show her to you," answers the Don, "what merit would there be in your confessing a truth so self-evident? The important thing is for you, without seeing her, to believe, confess, affirm, swear, and defend that truth."[14]

On the rare instances when Don Quixote wants to forget about a story, the author and Sancho stand at the ready. In the case of the fulling hammer discovery, the knight disagrees with Sancho who thinks the adventure a laughing matter and a good story as well. "I do not deny that what happened to us has its comical aspects, but it is best not to tell the story for not everyone is wise enough to see the point of the thing."[15] Of course, the story has already been told.

Because Don Quixote and even more so, his squire, have been so loyal to their adventures, defending them against all imitations, the story lives on. When the bachelor suggests that "there are some who have read the book who say that they would have been glad if the authors had forgotten a few of the innumerable cudgelings which Senõr Don Quixote received in the course of his various encounters," Sancho protests: "But that is where the truth of the story comes in."[16]

Throughout the book, Sancho must keep a sharp eye on his story which is being continually undermined by his master's enemies. A false manuscript, Don Juan tells the pair, finds Don Quixote no longer in love with Dulcinea and treats Sancho not as droll so much as a glutton and simpleton. But Sancho assures those who read the false story that he is the real Sancho whose "drolleries come faster than rain,"[17] that his master is the real Don Quixote who protects widows and orphans and undoes wrongs.

Vigilant as well is Don Quixote, who saves his story by sabotaging the rip-off. The false history tells how the knight participated in a tournament in Saragossa. "For that reason," said Don Quixote, "I will not set foot in Saragossa, but will let the world see how this new historian lies, by showing people that I am not the Don Quixote of whom he is speaking."[18] The knight knows well which story belongs to him.

When, in Dinesen's "The Immortal Story", Mr. Clay is unfaithful to the story by trying to force other characters, which he has brought to life, into a story of his own – "You walk and move at my bidding. You are, in reality, two young, strong and lusty jumping-jacks within this old hand of mine,"[19] – the results are predictably disastrous. No more successful is J. M. Coetzee's author Elizabeth Costello in the game novel *Slow Man*, whose character, Paul Rayment, objects to her authority: "'You treat me like a puppet…You treat every one like a puppet. You make up stories and bully us into playing them out for you." But Elizabeth Costello needs Paul Rayment as much as he needs her. He brings her to life.[20]

She wishes to make up another Don Quixote and Sancho with him. "Think of Don Quixote. *Don Quixote* is not about a man sitting in a rocking chair bemoaning the dullness of La Mancha. It is about a man who claps a basin on his head and clambers onto the back of his faithful old plough-horse and sallies forth to do great deeds." But at the end, when Elizabeth asks Paul to travel over hill and dale with her, he, who has no loyalty to any story, refuses. "I am of no use to you…of no value. Too pale, too cold, too frightened. What made you choose me? Why do you stay with me?"[21]

Calvino's Ludmilla confesses that "The novel I would most like to read at this moment should have as its driving force only the desire to narrate, to pile stories upon stories, without trying to impose a philosophy of life on you, simply allowing you to observe its own growth, like a tree, an entangling, as if of branches and leaves…."[22] But unlike Jacques' narrator, who marvels at "How easy it is to make up stories,"[23] Ludmilla does not ever have the chance to be faithful to the stories, even if she so desired, for Calvino hangs them in the air. Never finished, they simply melt into other narratives. Our only recourse is to sigh with McEwan's Briony: "How quickly the story was over."[24]

The Author

Never was author more powerful than Sheherazade who could, through her stories, prevent her husband, the king of Samarkind, from killing her. Today there seem to be no regrets that the author, erstwhile master of the house, solicitous towards his readers, engaged in the telling of his story, in love with many of his characters, is a helpless pawn of the reader, his characters no longer under his control, his story at the mercy of the audience.

The ideal good storyteller, says Willa Cather, is "observant, truthful, and kindly."[1] And pretend as he will to lightheartedly give over his task, Fielding is, in truth, the perfect host in *Joseph Andrews*, informing us that we need read no more than we like. When he finishes expressing a thought, he asks the reader to please proceed with the story. And if the author must bring up another part of the story, he will leave his characters together for a time while he entertains us with other matters.[2]

Early on, Sterne's Tristram addresses us as "my dear friend and companion." And as we proceed farther with him, "the slight acquaintance which is now beginning betwixt us, will grow into familiarity; and that, unless one of us is in fault, will terminate in friendship."[3] We, (and that includes those whom he addresses wryly as my lord, my lady, you critics), are to allow him to tell the story in his own way, and as we jog along, we may laugh at him or with him, but we should keep our temper. Were he to be given a kingdom, like Sancho, he would wish it one "of hearty laughing subjects."[4]

Not that Sterne and Diderot are above teasing and frustrating us. Companionship does not mean, of course, that they are prohibited from catching the reader off-guard. They are both nervy and playful, making full use of their arbitrary powers. Jacques' narrator tells the reader he does not know what he is talking about,[5] and Tristram would tear the next page out of his book if he thought the Reader was able "to form the least judgment or probable conjecture" about what was on it. He confesses there is "a strong propensity in me to begin this chapter very nonsensically, and I will not balk my fancy."[6] But the play is genial in an age of play.

Less genial than Tristram is Diderot's narrator, who bullies, taunts and teases us, his characters and his stories. In introducing Jacques' master, he describes him as "A passionate man like you, Reader. A curious man like you, Reader. A questioning man like you, Reader. A nuisance like you, Reader,"[7] all of which sounds very much like Dostoevsky's growling underground man. "I have been rude to you" cannot make the Reader feel in any way a companion. "To speak to you frankly, Reader, I find that you are the more wicked of the two of us. How satisfied would I be if it were as easy for me to protect myself from your calumny as it is for you to protect yourself from the boredom or the danger of my work."[8]

But even here, there is a big difference between the way Jacques, irreverent and clever in the Beaumarchais tradition, with a special relationship to his "master," is engaged fully in the society around him, and Dostoevsky's anti-hero, much more akin to (and a progenitor of) the modern tone and temperament, who, hiding in his hole, has neither family nor engagement. His "relationships" are all of the sickest sort, with his belittled servant, his "mistress," and a group of students from his university days whom he cannot abide and who humiliate him. In short, an unpleasant man and a bad storyteller.[9]

It might be that Tristram would like to abandon the book and his characters altogether but he cannot do so because he honors his responsibilities. "Let us leave, if possible, myself; – But 'tis impossible – I must go along with you to the end of the work."[10] Which is not to say he ignores the advantage of what freedom the text gives him "entering upon my uncle Toby's amours a fortnight before their existence," or handing the reins to another by calling upon a passing critic or his friends to help move his story along, not destroy it. "So then, friend! You have got my father and my uncle Toby off the stairs, and seen them to bed? – And how did you manage it? – You dropp'd a curtain at the stairs foot – I thought you had no other way for it – Here's a crown for your trouble."[11]

Jacques' "double" – Diderot's narrator – luxuriates in his compositional freedom. What is to prevent me from putting the coach in a ditch, or to have coaches crashing into one another, or to stage sword play, he asks. And, if you don't like that, what is to prevent me from doing all sorts of outrageous acts, even raising a character from the dead?[12]

But his patience wears thin as the demands on his resources increase. "And what is this, Reader? One love story after another? That makes one, two, three, four love stories I've told you and three or four more still to come."[13] Cranky and seemingly "irresponsible," he anticipates the questions of his readers: -"How did they meet? By chance like everyone else. What were their names? What's that got to do with you? Where were they coming from? From the nearest place. Where were they going to? Does anyone ever really know where they are going to" etc.[14] But in the end, the narrator fulfills his obligation to the reader honorably by continuing Jacques' story to its happy conclusion, the forlorn master once more united with his irreplaceable servant, and the servant united with his love Denise.

Whatever else one might say, the narrators used by Sterne or Diderot turn out to be, in their defiant ways, reliable. And this is the greatest service the author can render the reader. Once again, it is Cervantes who shows us how this is done, even in the wake of narrators within narrators, stories within stories, a pattern which leads post-modern critics to mistakenly, in my estimation, read the author's legerdemain as debunking authorship and authority.[15]

Cervantes, who calls his novel "the child of my brain," starts the ball rolling with no central authority – "certain authors say that his first adventure was that of Puerto Lapice, while others state that it was that of the windmills; but in this particular instance I am in a position to affirm what I have read in the annals of La Mancha, etc." Soon, however, the narrative runs dry and he must search out a continuation, which he finds in an Arabic manuscript. And though the Moorish author Hamete Benengeli becomes the strong chief narrator, he must depend upon a translator whom Cervantes hires.[16] And, of course, there are other authors along the way, the tellers of tales, the plagiarists, and, in the tradition of the times, the prologue with its advisors, censors, editors. Even the characters themselves talk of providing their author with adventures.

Cervantes provides an extra complication of a narrative filtered through Don Quixote's imagination, in which the changing of shapes engendered by an evil enchantress "Leads me to fear the history of my exploits, which they tell me has been printed, may be the work of some magician who is my enemy, in which case he would have set down one thing in place of another...."[17] But none of these narratives is introduced with the intent of seriously misleading the reader, as game novels are so inclined to do.

Though the first narrator holds no Christian love for Arabs, and calls Cid Hamete, who blesses the mighty Allah! "a hound of an author," he sees to it that he also swears "as a Catholic Christian" which leads the translator to explain that although he is a Moor he will adhere to the truth in the same way a Christian would in taking an oath.[18] At Don Quixote's death bed, the curate asks the notary to be a witness to the fact that Alonso Quijano, known as Don Quixote, had indeed expired, and he does so to prevent any other author but Cid Hamete Benengeli from falsely resurrecting him and continuing his exploits. In any case, Cervantes trusts him. Hamete is continually being cited as the recognized authority, and a reliable historian. All of us, Cervantes tells us, "ought to be grateful to him, its original author, for the pains he has taken in setting forth every detail of [this history], leaving out nothing, however slight, but making everything very clear and plain. He describes thoughts, reveals fancies, answers unasked questions, clears up doubts, and settles arguments. In short, he satisfies on every minutest point the curiosity of the most curious."[19]

The horsemen who were friends of Roque Guinart greet not the false Don Quixote, "not the fictitious, not the apocryphal one that we read of in mendacious histories that have appeared of late, but the true and legitimate one, the real one that Cid Hamete Benengeli, flower of historians, has portrayed for us."[20] Still, Cervantes generously allows the translator, the author, the readers to make their own informed judgments. The translator, for instance, desires, as he sets down the fifth chapter, to make it plain that he looks upon it as apocryphal, since in it Sancho Panza does not speak in a manner expected of one with his limited intelligence. And Cid Hamete is allowed to have personal opinions, as well – "the jesters were as crazy as their victims and…the duke and duchess were not two fingers breadth removed from being fools when they went to so much trouble to make sport of the foolish."[21] Finally, the history is finished and Cervantes, who has called himself Don Quixote's "stepfather" in the prologue, takes center stage once more.

As the world became more treacherous in its complexities, pressuring the story, the need for narrators to be reliable was all the greater. Conrad's Marlowe honors the fact of the story even if the mystery is beyond him. Henry James has his share of unreliable narrators in his shorter works but his purpose, far from meaning to deceive us, is to show us how they deceive themselves. And Svevo's Zeno, proud of his unreliability, who, with his inventive lies and wit, makes people laugh, is reliable despite his exaggerations and inventions precisely because he lets us know what he is up to: "...I myself could not open my mouth without misrepresenting things or people," Zeno confesses, "for otherwise I should have seen no use in talking at all."[22]

The reader depends upon the reliable author, but the characters do as well. Fielding not only loves his characters but wants us to become intimate with them. Those who have as great an affection for Mr. Wilson as the author does will rejoice at seeing him walking through the parish, "as it may give them hopes of seeing him again."[23]

At a later age, of course, the expression of such love must be more reticent. Hardy loves his Tess in such a way that, as Irving Howe describes it, he brings her to the point where neither he nor we are qualified to judge her.[24] James uses his prefaces to show his devotion to Isabella and Milly. Joyce is obliged to confess his through parody: "And sir Leopold that was the goodliest guest that ever sat in scholars' hall and that was the meekest man and the kindest that had husbandly hand under hen and that was the very truest knight of the world...."[25]

Though the author is head of the House of Fiction, he has so much trust in his characters he is quite willing to give them some freedom. "It all comes back, in fine," Henry James famously remarks, "to that respect for the liberty of the subject which [the author] should be willing to name as the great sign of the painter of the first order...."[26] Fielding is loathe to make Joseph Andrews read his speech on charity in the next chapter, "for we scorn to betray him into any such reading, without first giving him warning,"[27] and Trollope makes space for the characters by carefully interpolating phrases such as "And yet I am inclined to think."

The more daring step is to give the reins of narrative to the character. Classical literature offers some grand examples. Athêna, who called Odysseus a contriver, like her, and lord knows he was, thought him also the best in plots and story-telling.[28] Odysseus listens to the Bard but he is one as well, so reliable a teller that Homer hands over a large section of his narrative to him, as Virgil does to Aeneas.

In fact, Virgil actually gives his hero a chance to prove his reliability. We remember when Aeneas tells King Evander of their common ancestry, he adds, as an aside, "if we can trust these tales." The reader, warned, does not then have to pay heed to D.H. Lawrence's honored advice: "Never trust the artist. Trust the tale."[29] The author even allows the arch story-spoilers, the Gods, to tell the story as well, story-tellers we are not disposed to question.

Like the classical heroes, Jacques plays his part while knowing how things will turn out. Diderot does not give him his independence without touching base with us, assuring us that he and Jacques are cooperating. "Everything which I have just told you, Reader, I was told by Jacques. I admit it to you because I do not like to take credit for the cleverness of others."[30]

The grand master of the tradition, Dickens, added complications by using, as narrator, a heroine who is not certain of the ending of her story, with obvious dramatic advantages. Esther Summerson of *Bleak House*, with her genuine puzzlement and saintly but suspect modesty, sometimes makes difficulties for the author, but remains loyal to him nonetheless. Still, the measure of autonomy the characters have gained will, ironically, in the long run, prove dangerous for the very novelistic genre they hold dear.

There are those, as well, who reject the heavy burden of narrative their authors put upon them. In the end, Huck Finn wants to go back to being a full-time character, for being a narrator has caused him a powerful lot of trouble, "so there ain't nothing more to write about, and I am rotten glad of it, because if I'd 'a' knowed what a trouble it was to make a book, I wouldn't 'a' tackled it, and ain't a-going to no more." Nevertheless, Huck gets the job done…and how!

When Sterne-Tristram changes the order of his chapters, he does so to teach the world "to let people tell their stories their own way."[31] This becomes interesting in the hands of a modern author like Ian McEwan, who has learned the lesson well in *Atonement*. Briony, whose fiction is known for its amorality,[32] is given leave to tell the story her own way.

But this narrator has her personal problems with guilt, and proceeds to jeopardize the story McEwan has set out for his characters. Briony's sister and lover do not survive the war but at the end of the book, she is determined to change that history. "I like to think that it isn't weakness or evasion, but a final act of kindness, a stand against oblivion and despair, to let my lovers live and to unite them at the end. I gave them happiness, but I was not so self-serving as to let them forgive me. Not quite, not yet...."

The dangers are present, we can see, for an unreliable narrator with plenty of subjective issues, to sabotage her author's intentions. We might say that the very subject of *Atonement* is precisely the problem of the character as author, whose own story is "writing itself around her."[33] We are moving to a place where the inter-relationship of author, story and character becomes highly problematic.

For all her difficulties, Briony has tried to steer us honestly. Nabokov's Kimbote, on the other hand, who does not ever have control of the truth of the story, renders *Pale Fire* a narrative of misreading. The author uses our hopelessly parallel and partial stories Calvino calls "the poor alphabets by which one human being believes at certain moments that he is reading another human being"[34] as his central theme. Kimbote assumes the poet John Shade will use as a catalytic agent of creativity "all the live, glamorous palpitating, shimmering material I have lavished upon him,"[35] the romance of Zembla and its king, when in fact, Shade is writing about his own travails. It is only a fluke (Kimbote calls his story a "fable of fate"[36]) in a world of crazy chance which, in the end, causes their narratives to cross. The author's pyrotechnics put a heavy strain on the story, which, in the novelistic tradition, was charged with bringing some order, pattern, mutuality to this world of partialities.

Not that the crazy Kimbote means to be unreliable. He admits with some unaccustomed awareness that his exalted admiration for John Shade was "enhanced by my awareness of [inferior people] not feeling what I felt, of their not seeing what I saw...."[37] But when Kimbote realizes how he has been misled by Shade, he refuses to give up his narrative. He sees himself still as the poet's keeper and preserver, for "without my notes Shade's text simply has no human reality at all since the human reality of such a poem as his...has to depend entirely on the reality of its author and his surroundings, attachments and so forth, a reality that only my notes can provide."[38] Kimbote as commentator at the end of the forward thinks he has the last word, but the joke is on the character. It is Nabokov who speaks last as the consummate unreliable author.

This is the game Pirandello plays, who prides himself on fooling his characters by casting them in their roles "in a certain drama while I present them as characters in another play which they don't know and don't suspect the existence of."[39] Now if the author is more intelligent than his text, an imbalance Kundera considers unacceptable,[40] what does this say about the novel as game where we can trust neither the teller nor the tale. The authors are too smart for their own good; they separate themselves from their text with deleterious results for the House of Fiction; respect no longer holds when the mind comes first.

The "essential function of art is moral" after all, Lawrence reminds us "not aesthetic, not decorative, not pastime and recreation." And it features not a didactic but "a passionate, implicit morality...a morality which changes the blood, rather than the mind. ... The mind follows later...." Why "purpose" and "passion" should have gotten separated "is a mystery."[41] Yorick recognizes this unfortunate separation in judging that his sermon came from the head and not the heart, but Tristram makes no such mistake. "I write a careless kind of a civil, nonsensical, good humoured Shandean book, which will do all your hearts good----And all your heads too...."[42]

In *Austerlitz*, a shallow novel about a very deep subject, Sebald's protagonist shows neither purpose nor passion. His friend describes Austerlitz' method which called for sitting sometimes hours at a time, "laying out these photographs, or others from his collection the wrong way up...and that then, one by one, he turned them over, always with a new sense of surprise at what he saw, pushing the pictures back and forth...until either there was nothing left but the gray tabletop, or he felt exhausted by the constant effort of thinking and remembering and had to rest on the ottoman."[43] Though there are various "tellers" of this story, the real author is chance itself, which does not oppose but trumps choice, in contrast to Hardy's novels where, though chance shows Providence no longer protects us in a post-Darwinian world, it is still pitted against desire.

Cortázar's Etienne explains the novelist Morelli's intentions: "You've probably noticed already that he gets less and less worried about joining the parts together, that business of one word's leading to another...." The novelist himself doesn't care at all. "You can read my book any way you want to!"[44] And why not? The underground man confesses that "It would be better if I myself believed in anything I had just written. I assure you most solemnly, gentlemen, that there is not a word I've just written I believe in! What I mean is that perhaps I do believe, but at the same time I cannot help feeling and suspecting for some unknown reason that I'm lying like a cobbler." In such a case, the writing of stories seems like "a corrective punishment."[45] Why not, then, simply throw in the towel. The author in Calvino's *If on a winter's night a traveler* does not even recognize his novel, which has taken on a life of its own. When his translator shows him a Japanese volume with his name on it, he leafs through it but can't figure out which of his books it is. "Even if you knew the language you wouldn't recognize the book," the translator says. "It's a book you have never written."[46]

The process of losing control of the story is most brilliantly portrayed by the nun in Calvino's fable *The Nonexistent Knight*. We remember that at the end of *Don Quixote*, Cervantes gives his pen the last word: "For me alone Don Quixote was born and I for him. It was for him to act, for me to write, and we two are one...." Tristram claims in jest his pen "governs me—I govern not it."[47] Sister Theodora's pen, on the other hand, has a life and a will entirely divorced from her and the character of Bradamante she becomes in her story. At one point "I long to hurry on with my story, tell it quickly, embellish every page with enough duels and battles for a poem but when I pause and start re-reading I realize that my pen has left no mark on the paper and the pages are blank." At another time, however, "the pen," (never my pen), "rushes on, urged by the same joy that makes me course the open road."[48]

John Barth's *Coming Soon!!!* is so self-referential, so metafictional, so hypertextual, we might wonder if the "author" even cares whether we read it or not. In any case, he is given the burden of choosing three different endings. In a review of this work, Jennifer Schuessler refers to a story by David Foster Wallace, one of whose characters calls such post-modern experimental fiction "novels about novelists writing novels about novelists."[49] (Remember Hazlitt's desire that authors should converse primarily with elite fellow authors, and the subject of their talk should be books?)[50]

Barth's calling up two of the world's greatest story-tellers – Odysseus and Scheherazade – simply awakens in us a terrible realization of the closing novelistic arc. Though his kind of fiction might already seem passé, there is nothing in the future which gives us confidence. The high table author has no more profession. From caring little for the truth of his story, it is no difficult task for the author to disappear altogether.

In *If on a winter's night a traveler*, Flannery recalls a theory Marana proposed to him, that "the author of every book is a fictitious character whom the existent author invents to make him the author of his fictions." Flannery would like to erase himself, "and find for each book another I, another voice, another name, to be reborn; but my aim is to capture in the book the illegible world, without center, without ego, without I."[51] We'll let Roland Barthes have the last word on what it means to be a deconstructed author: "Who speaks is not who writes and who writes is not who is."[52]

The Characters

Once the story is in place, Dinesen's Cardinal tells us, "the characters will gather."[1] Although, as we have seen, characters in the epic and novel tradition are often given authorial responsibilities, with various degrees of autonomy, it is the story that renders the characters immortal and they know it. When Thomas Mann's Joseph remarks with gratitude and wonder "what a good story I am in",[2] he understands that it will preserve his role, as it has preserved the role of a long line of characters, deserving and undeserving alike. "An immortal story immortalizes its hero" says the Cardinal. This is true, of course, for Hector and Achilles, but it is also true for Ali Baba, who is, in himself "nothing more than an honest woodcutter," an "adequate hero" who resides in "a very great story."[3] The magic formula "Open, Sesame" is pure luck. There is no earning or learning. Magical fortune comes to Aladdin, not a particularly worthy person, as well.

Oliver Twist, in his apparent passivity, may seem to have much in common with these fairy tale figures; hardly surprising since, as Walter Benjamin observes, the fairy-tale lives on in all stories.[4] Secret births and legacies are staples of Dickens' novels as much as they are in the tale of "The Singing Bird," where birth bestows beauty and heroism on the lucky recipient. Aladdin becomes a different person and a gentleman after he receives riches. But *Oliver Twist* is a "new secular drama of salvation," in which, as Steven Marcus observes, "conduct has become the only means of deliverance: if someone behaves like a gentleman, some day he can hope to awaken and find he has been one all along."[5] The characters of the traditional novels are not passive recipients. As Dickens matures, his characters in works like *Martin Chuzzlewit*, *Dombey and Son*, *Great Expectations*, *Our Mutual Friend* attain spiritual depth more through learning and growing than through grace. In short, they become Bildungsroman heroes and heroines, liberated and educated, in a way the epic or fairy-tale hero never can be.

Dinesen's Cardinal holds his high office of keeper and watchman of the story with the sacred knowledge that "to its human characters there is salvation in nothing else in the universe."[6] And it is not surprising that those nineteenth-century novels which carry a salvific melodramatic strain are among our greatest. A story with as many coincidences as *Oliver Twist* is entirely credible[7] because these coincidences carry that sense of life Dickens had at his fingertips as a resident of nineteenth-century England. By contrast, the literary coincidences in contemporary novels, worked up in a void, seem hokey and labored, improbable and desperate.

We can hardly be surprised that as the novel *Don Quixote* embodies all genres, the character Don Quixote embodies three kinds of literary heroes: the epic – had he been born in the age of Troy, "all I should have had to do would have been to slay Paris, and all the ensuing misfortunes would have been avoided",[8] the picaresque – traveling over hill and dale, meeting adventures, stopping at inns, and finally, a true Bildungsroman figure as well. Unlike the epic hero, in this role he must carry the moral burden of the novelistic tradition. In the epic, Ortega reminds us, "The men of Homer belong to the same world as their desires," whereas Don Quixote takes an active role in his desire to "reform reality," to alter "the course of things." He must tear himself away from the habitual and the customary, inventing a new world, though he is destined thereby to live a life of "perpetual suffering".[9] His name may be in the history books as a courteous, respected, brave man of arms but in expecting triumph, he meets humiliation. Nevertheless, like his hero Amadis, he will attempt great things or die attempting them.[10]

Don Quixote does differ from most of the Bildungsroman heroes in one important respect. In the end, he dies to his story. Vanquished by the arm of another, he returns to his village to live a pastoral life for a year, which Sancho reads as a victory for his master, the greatest victory that could be desired, that is a victory over himself.[11] But he is mistaken, for the greatest victory has already been his master's loyalty to the story. Sansón assures Don Quixote that "no sooner do folks see some skinny nag than they at once cry, 'There goes Rocinante!'" and as soon as one lays the story down, there is always another reader who will pick it up.[12] The knight of the mournful countenance, Sancho Panza, Dulcinea, belong to us. (Svevo's Zeno offers a modern version of this "victory." He has spent his life inventing memory pictures and fantasies. "Now alas, I believe in them no longer, to my sorrow, and know that it was not the pictures that fled, but my eyes from which a veil was lifted, so that they looked out again on real space, where there is no room for spirits."[13] To which we say, as readers, oh, but the inventive Zeno with his beguiling stories and exaggerations belongs to us.)

Even though the knight may seem a questionable fit for a Bildungsroman, we have no trouble placing him, who has "ways of adjusting everything,"[14] within the central moral tradition of the novel. But what do we say about the ever troublesome square pegs in a round hole, the eccentrics of *Tristram Shandy*? In fact, Sterne's characters clearly belong strongly to the moral tradition as well because they do correct, reform and expand "the ethical ideal,"[15] which Ortega tells us is a primary duty of the moral life, simply by being. When Trim tells Toby he failed to offer a purse to an old soldier and his son because he had no orders to do so, uncle Toby replies "True...thou didst very right Trim, as a soldier, – but certainly very wrong as a man."[16]

Who would not agree with Hazlitt that "Uncle Toby is one of the finest compliments ever paid to human nature." And Coleridge observes that in uncle Toby's freeing of the fly we see "how individual character may be given...humanity."[17] (Remember Sancho's distaste for hunting which "consists in killing an animal that has done no harm whatever.")[18] What he fears most, uncle Toby tells Trim, is "doing a wrong thing."[19] Tristram himself knows "that the lesson of universal good-will then taught and imprinted by my uncle Toby, has never been worn out of my mind"[20] and it was learned by all around him. Nor does uncle Toby's military obsession give the lie to his gentleness. Not only does Toby tell Trim that he loves mankind more than either glory or pleasure, but he views a knowledge of arms as a furtherance of good and quiet in the world, particularly the kind practiced on the bowling-green.[21]

Though Joyce came at the far end of the classical novel, he still found a way for his central character to carry the moral burden. Bloom's humanity seems closest to Toby's as he expresses his sympathy for animals in pain, for doctors who work so hard without our gratitude, and for the patients as well. He is sorry for the blind man crossing the street, and angry that we assume deformed people are less clever than we are. Typically, he finds it unfair that there are no urinals for women.[22] (After all, Molly was first attracted to him, she says, because she saw that he understood or felt what a woman is.) It is Bloom's natural goodness in putting himself down for five shillings which catches the notice of Mr. Power: "...without a word either," and of Nolan: "I'll say there is much kindness in the jew, he quoted, elegantly."[23]

Through the ages, the great protagonists have had the task of defying the doubters of their narratives. Don Quixote's niece is blunt. "And yet, to think that you could be so blind and foolish as to try to make out that you are a hero when you are really an old man, that you are strong when you are sick, that you are able to straighten out the wrongs of the world when you yourself are bent with age...."[24] Fermina's daughter pronounces love at her mother-in-law's age "revolting",[25] whereupon

Fermina sails away with Ariza, surrounded by cholera and environmental degradation.

And they are asked to fashion material for their authors as well. Don Quixote's remorse on his death bed that he has provided Hamete Benengeli with so many absurdities to put into his writing is canceled out by his previous pride and by Sancho's in supplying adventures for their author and their eagerness to have as many witnesses as possible so that their exploits would be put down in writing. The characters are more than willing to feed the story to their historian by living it. "My master and I," Sancho tells the Moorish gentleman, "will supply [our author] with enough stuff, ready at hand, in the way of adventures and other happenings, to make not only one second part but a hundred of them."[26]

On the other hand, Coetzee's author in *Slow Man*, Elizabeth Costello, must push her reluctant character, Paul Rayment, into a life that would give her some drama to work with. Though he rebels, Paul finally offers her some material about his marriage. "You can use it to illustrate my character, or not, as you wish."[27]

In "Six characters in search of an author," Pirandello's Father understands that "whoever has the luck to be born a living character can also laugh at death. He will never die!"[28] It is important to note, however, that the characters he cites all had loving and responsible authors. "Who was Sancho Panza? Who was Don Abbondio? But they live forever because, as live germs, they have the luck to find a fertile matrix, an imagination which knew how to raise and nourish them, make them live through all eternity!"[29]

The Father describes what he thinks is the chief attribute of a character succinctly: The Director's reality "changes all the time, like everyone else's but ours does not, sir. You see, that is the difference. It does not change, it cannot ever change or be otherwise because it is already fixed, it is what is, just that, forever...."[30] But suppose these characters become what William James reminds us we all are, "the very personages in the world drama."[31] Now that's a problem.

And it arises from the need, always the need, for the author to move forward. Why not, Pirandello asks in his preface, have them detached from me, live on their own, acquire "voice and movement," become dramatic characters who must learn to defend themselves in the struggle for existence they wage with me. Their story walks out of the front door of fiction (or drama) and wanders about in "real" life, beyond the proscenium. It isn't as if Pirandello's six characters are anxious to destroy their House. But when characters come before story, we know there is going to be trouble ahead. Now Pirandello must follow through on his experiment. Though they plead with him in his study to write their story, he is no longer interested. They must act out their own drama while the prompter records it.[32]

Well, you say, remember how relieved Sterne's Tristram was to get his characters out of the way – "All my heroes are off my hands – 'tis the first time I have had a moment to spare"[33] – yet we know he is anything but serious; he has no intention of leaving. He is making use of his time to write a preface. When we look at *Shira*, however, the experimental last unfinished novel of S. Y. Agnon, we find that the author's and the character's indifference swears no fealty to the House of Fiction whatsoever. As for the elusive heroine, "...we won't be looking for you. Not today...Tomorrow afternoon we might perhaps go and see where you live. If we find you, good. If we don't find you, it's your fault for not sitting and waiting for us." Shira "went wherever she went,"[34] and there will be no consequences if she stays rebellious. No longer can we count on the promise that "where the story is, the characters will gather."

Once Pirandello's six characters have been forced to become their own authors, they cannot play their roles and must find actors to do so. They would like to tell their story in the absence of their author, but that is not so easy since "the whole world can imagine [them] in innumerable situations other than those the author thought to place [them] in,"[35] thus opening the door to the reader as author. For McEwan's character-writer Briony, who dislikes her role and the story her author has put her in but is not yet ready to give up her place in the House of Fiction or sabotage her organizing powers, the way out might be to move into "a richer story" and "prove herself worthy of it,"[36] even if she is disloyal to her creator.

But the underground man, proudly identifying himself as the anti-hero, without character or compass, could, of course, never be an organizing force. "A novel must have a hero," he says. "I seemed to have deliberately gathered together all the characteristics of an anti-hero…," a man who lacks "moral courage."[37] This is not the "bully" who appears in virtually every novel of the great tradition. Somewhat premature in his declaration, he is, in fact, on target for the modern novel. "Yes, a man of the nineteenth century must be, and is indeed morally bound to be, above all, a characterless person." So much so that it is a pleasure when people call him a loafer, for it would mean "that a positive definition had been found for me and that there was something one could say about me."[38] Regretting he could not even become an insect, he calls to mind Kafka's more "privileged" Gregor Samsa.

This "characterlessness" has dire consequences for the House of Fiction since, as Harold Bloom puts it, great literature "fully establishes and augments an autonomous self" in the reader.[39] Hadn't Dinesen's Cardinal told us that "within our whole universe the story has authority to answer that cry of heart of its characters, that one cry of heart of each of them: Who am I?"[40] Now who can forget the great cry Don Quixote utters at the beginning of his adventures: "I know who I am and who I may be if I choose…"?[41] And Sancho knows who he is, as well, having to vouch for his own reality when a false Sancho appears in the ersatz story of their adventures in print.

But what to think when, at the home of the Duke and Duchess, the historian pulls back a curtain by telling us astonishingly of Don Quixote that "…indeed it may be said this was first time he really and wholly believed himself to be a true knight-errant and not a fanciful one, for here he was being treated in the very same manner as knights-errant in ages past, according to the storybooks he had read."[42] Or of the bargaining of fantasies as Sancho weaves his story about flying close to the heavens and sneaking a peek at the tiny earth after which Don Quixote whispers in his ear "Sancho…if you want us to believe what you saw in Heaven, then you must believe me when I tell you what I saw in the Cave of Montesinos. I need say no more."[43] The knight possesses, in fact, what Aristotle recognizes as a legitimate quality of a character, to be consistently inconsistent.[44] The poignancy of his cry, then, is demonstrated by the fact that he does indeed know who he is and at the same time, insists on being what he might be, a beautiful moral dialectic which puts *Don Quixote*, the mother of all game novels, squarely in the Bildungsroman column and which recognizes Don Quixote as a hero of substance.

The significant difference between the hero of the Bildungsroman and the anti-hero of modern literature is that the hero does not only find himself, but, as Jacques Barzun points out, more precisely makes himself.[45] This is impossible for the anti-hero who has all he can handle just learning how to be; everything has to start "from scratch" since he has no social or historical identification or support. It is the difference between David Copperfield, who wonders what he is to become, and the underground man, who "...should never become a different man... because as a matter of fact there was nothing I could change into...."[46]

In *Hopscotch*, Horacio's friend tells him he is like something disembodied, "you're a will in the form of a weather vane, up there."[47] The danger of "characterlessness" is not only a diminishment of interest in the story for the reader but more lethal, the character's lack of interest in the story, since he has been assigned no part in it and the authors have not taken the trouble to keep him alive. In fact, current authors seem to have so little interest or ability to imagine a character they must borrow from real life its famous artists, philosophers, scientists, world leaders: Henry and William James, Virginia Woolf, Dostoevsky, Shakespeare, Schubert, Mozart, Shostakovich, Heisenberg, Bohr and Einstein appear in films, novels, plays.

There are Japanese robot toys that allow us to program in the personality type we want. Or none if we so desire. In popular ensemble films, the young fill the screen with their faceless bodies, often engaging in intercourse of the most mechanical sort. You have but to mix the characters around and come up with a different story. In Calvino's *If on a winter's night a traveler* the protagonist of a novel watches as another boy occupies his room and possesses everything in it – "an outsider was taking my place, was becoming me...just as I was about to become him, to take his place among the things and people of his life."[48]

Sebald arranges for the narrator to find out something about Austerlitz by chance because "it was almost impossible to talk to him about anything personal...."[49] And Austerlitz relates what story he has to a nameless companion. (The nameless companion in Henry James' "Altar of the Dead" serves, by contrast, to highlight precisely the fatal loss of identity in the central protagonist.) Nameless as well are Palomar's few friends who call each other to check on bird patterns.[50] Nameless the "I" in the opening pages of *If on a winter's night a traveler*, who tells us it's risky to identify with the narrator, risky for you the reader and for him the author.[51]

Nabokov's chess champion Luzhin in *The Defense* represents a negative of the Bildungsroman hero. His unique strategy is known as the Luzhin defense, but his novel as game becomes his game as novel. Significantly, when, in the end, he decides the only solution is for him "to drop out of the game" through an open window, his entire name is shouted. "'Aleksandr Ivanovich', 'Aleksandr Ivanovich,' roared several voices. But there was no Aleksandr Ivanovich."

It is not difficult to move from namelessness to the masks Pirandello's performers wear, each representing, (back to the mythic gods), a character's "fundamental sentiment, thus: remorse Father, revenge stepdaughter, disdain son, grief mother."[52] Or, looking forward, characters become cartoon fantasies in computer games, comic books, graphic novels and films.

The "I" of a character can become simply an eye. Austerlitz tells the narrator about his visit with Vera: "...I see the two of us as it were disembodied, or more precisely, reduced to the unnaturally enlarged pupils of our eyes...."[53] An eye is Mr. Palomar, as well, who "has decided that his chief activity will be looking at things from the outside... To do this, he has to face each time problems of selection, exclusion, hierarchies of preference; he soon realizes he is spoiling everything, as always when he involves his own ego and all the problems he has with his own ego."[54] Better to take advantage of some time when the world "wants to look and to be looked at" just as Mr. Palomar is passing by.

No loss of will could be more severe. In contemplating the stars, Mr. Palomar "has become accustomed to considering himself an anonymous and incorporeal dot, almost forgetting that he exists; to deal now with human beings, he cannot help involving himself and he no longer knows where his self is to be found."⁵⁵

If Palomar, with no inner being, exists through his observations of the material world, Dostoevsky's underground man shows us what happens when the outer world fails us. "By the way, what does a decent chap talk about with the greatest possible pleasure? Answer: about himself. Very well, so I will talk about myself."⁵⁶ What the great novels did so effectively was to strike a balance between inner and outer mindfulness, knowing the self and knowing the world; even more effectively, these were often set against one another in a characteristic dialectical formation. Proust and Joyce manage to find intense outside worlds despite their interior monologues.

A perversion of the mid-eighteenth-century Richardson novel, where, as Kundera points out, "in quest for self, [the character] was forced to turn away from the visible world of action and examine the invisible interior life,"⁵⁷ shows up as the close psychological analysis that takes over the modern novel and becomes clinical. (Were it not for magical realism, Ariza's fanatic love for Fermina in *Love in the Time of Cholera* might otherwise be considered a disorder in the way Victoria's forty-year mourning for Albert would be known today as ESG, excessive grief syndrome.)⁵⁸ The ego becomes separated from the body, far from Tristram's history of himself *ab ovo* and leaves fiction for memoirs and case histories. Lee Siegel argues that Freud's ideas were deadly for the novelistic characters who became nothing more than id, ego, super-ego, "the forces of repression, displacement and neurosis." What character after the war, he asks, "has the memorableness of a Gatsby, a Nick Adams, a Baron Charlus, a Leopold Bloom, a Settembrini."⁵⁹

Hints of the fragmented ego appear in *Tristram Shandy* and *Rameau's Nephew* but, as we have made clear, within the context of a readable universe, the characters remain flesh and blood. In his early career, we recall, Calvino had not given up on a constructed ego, the need for wholeness in our identities, by showing us the dangers of our separate good and evil halves in his fable *The Cloven Viscount*. It is the author's ambiguity that fattens the character and makes it whole. For the evil half slashes everything in sight and the good half causes unintentional bad consequences. The citizens felt "lost between an evil and a virtue equally inhuman."⁶⁰ But the evil half had his own reasonable morality in his deviant way, for his desire to halve everyone and thing came from his desire to free us from obtuse and ignorant wholeness. "I was whole and all things were natural and confused to me, stupid as the air; I thought I was seeing all and it was only the outside rind" because "beauty and knowledge and justice only exist in what has been cut to shreds." Once the viscount is put together again, having had "the experience of both halves each on its own, he was bound to be wise."⁶¹

The fullness of the whole character remains in the strong moral tradition of the novel. Only united could there emerge a reasonably kind, compassionate and decent knight, with wisdom gained by having been split into two. For by being halved, "One understands the sorrow of every person and thing in the world at its own incompleteness. I was whole and did not understand, and moved about deaf and unfeeling amid the pain and sorrow all round us… It's not only me, Pamela, who am a split being, but you and everyone else too. Now I have a fellowship…with all the mutilated and incomplete things in the world."⁶²

In creating the cloven viscount, Calvino has gone some way to deconstructing the ego but changes course when he successfully puts the two halves together again in a stronger ego. Later, however, he pursues the deconstruction in earnest. Mr. Palomar, swimming in the ocean, imagines three egos conflicting within him, already a bodiless observer, and a character in *If on a winter's night a traveler* wants to multiply himself by mirrored reflections, all at different angles so that no one can catch him or see the real man. "I want to conceal, in the midst of so many illusory ghosts of myself, the true me…."⁶³ But there are few true me's in modern fiction.

The Bildungsroman featured the evolution of character, while evolution in Calvino's *Cosmicomiche* means simply eons of darkness, elemental life in the water, dinosaurs traveling through valleys and plains and contemporary travelers catching trains and planes – not to take the fun away, but simply to show how character becomes irrelevant.

The deconstruction of character must obviously be accompanied by a total lack of emotional interest in other human beings. Austerlitz sees the shapes of discrete things through photography, but "it never seemed to me right to turn the viewfinder of my camera on people." The narrator can only study "the black and white photographs which, one day, would be all that was left of [Austerlitz's] life."[64] (This is a variant on the underground man's way of talking about life as if he were reading from a book.)

One might be tempted to place Zeno at the beginning of a long post-modern line of non-listeners and riffers, (Bellow, Roth), though he observes that many people learn best by listening to themselves – "talkativeness was an absolute necessity to me."[65] Zeno's father complains that he won't be able to tell his son what he really thinks because he "always make[s] game of everything."[66] But even his one-way ticket performances are lovable – "My whimsical chatter amused everyone..." – because he makes game of himself as well: "...the world would certainly be less disagreeable if there were more people like me in it."[67]

The great novels depended upon listening as well as talking and the loss of such interactions has become a hallmark of modern artistic endeavors. When we look at Manet's "Dejeuner sur l'herbe" of 1866, we see a group of figures engaged in conversation. Engaged, as well, the group in Renoir's "Luncheon of the Boating Party," 1880-1. But only five years later, Seurat's "A Sunday Afternoon on La Grande Jatte" of 1884-6, shows us figures all lost in their own thoughts. Edvard Munch's 1899-1900 "Dance of Life" looks more like a dance of death, "no longer, as it was for Renoir, a carefree occasion of joy in the warm contact of bodies...but rather a chilly, morbid, macabre affair,"[68] and his clichéd 1893 "Scream", with its two background figures on the bridge unconcerned with the anxiety in the foreground, seems to give up all hope of reciprocity.

Through the thick settings of the great novels, there was always an active give and take. (Once we get to Kafka it is the experience of not sharing which is paramount,[69] but he is both prescient and *sui generis*.) In the novel of game, we find the perfect conduit for social indifference and unreliability. As Calvino's Marco Polo says, "There is no language without deceit."[70] One does not even have to show up. Why waste effort at real conversation when the imagination can do the work. "At this point Kublai Khan interrupted him, or imagined interrupting him, or Marco Polo imagined himself interrupted... All this so that Marco Polo could explain or imagine explaining or be imagined explaining or succeed finally in explaining to himself that what he sought was always something lying ahead."[71]

Everyone in *Don Quixote* listens willingly or unwillingly – even Rocinante and Sancho's gray. Sancho tries to tell a story of a goatherd when he is interrupted by his master and told to tell his story directly. When Sancho insists upon his customary way, the Don understands that fate has decreed he must listen. The natural interruptions of interchange are exaggerated in *Tristram Shandy* and *Jacques le fataliste*, but stories are being told and heard. *If on a winter's night a traveler*, with its synecdochal title, however, features stories that are evanescent, the interruptions permanent.

William Gaddis' novel *JR* combines bodiless characters with a consistent pattern of not listening. If the eponymous character, a mere child, were to be seen, it would dash all confidence in this hugely successful entrepreneur so he conducts his business strictly through the phone and through surrogates. His patter never stops: "...this here bond and stock stuff you don't see anybody, you don't know anybody only in the mail and the telephone because that's how they do it nobody has to see anybody...they're just selling it back and forth for some voice that told them on the phone." If you manage to speak to JR in person, "he doesn't look at you but it's not as though, not like he's hiding something. He looks like he's trying to fit what you're saying into some utterly different, some world you don't know anything about...."[72]

The phone "conversations," throughout the book, are carried on by a number of people very difficult to distinguish. To make matters more bewildering, they are rarely finished. A voice often reaches the wrong number or is speaking to the wrong person at the right number. Phones are picked up and hung up in equal measure. Phones are constantly ringing; there is a fear lovemaking will be interrupted. A voice from a radio cannot be turned off because it cannot be found under a pile of junk. And the junk itself significantly consists primarily of unopened packages, unread mail and brochures. Messages do not reach their destinations. Everything is indirect and unrelated, a disparate mess.

Gibbs tries to explain his work to Bast but has to keep telling him to listen. Not even the operator listens. "Hello...? It's what operator...? No but I haven't talked any overtime, I haven't even... No I didn't even, I don't even know anybody in Union Falls and I... But I don't have sixty cents, even wait wait wait, operator? Operator I wanted to call New York and I just happened to pick up the...but I can't dial again I just, I don't have the right change... ,"[73] etc. The last line of the novel belongs to JR and it is a universal one: "Hey, you listening?" Sure, to cell phones and iPods in today's Gaddis land.

Of Mr. Palomar, we might ask, hey, you talking? He wonders if two blackbirds he observes understand each other, or is it simply a dialogue between the deaf.[74] (In Austerlitz, Sebald decides to relinquish dialogue altogether and Cortázar's Horacio Oliveira understands that "Everybody thinks he's talking about something he has in common with everybody else." But this is likely to be simply "a mutual misunderstanding.")[75] Palomar wonders if it is possible for one person to understand another. In society, he thinks about what he is about to say or not say, and what others will say or not say and decides to bite his tongue.[76] In fact, Mr. Palomar wants to talk about the albino gorilla he has seen in the zoo, but no one wants to listen. Just as the wordless gorilla has his tire, so "we all turn in our hands an old, empty tire through which we try to reach some final meaning, which words cannot achieve."[77]

It is in *If on a winter's night a traveler* that Calvino pushes the impossibility of communication to its limits. From the beginning, "the lights of the station and the sentences you are reading seem to have the job of dissolving more than of indicating the things that surface from a veil of darkness and fog... I am the man who comes and goes between the bar and the telephone booth. Or, rather: that man is called "I" and you know nothing else about him, just as this station is called only 'station' and beyond it there exists nothing except the unanswered signal of a telephone ringing in a dark room of a distant city."[78] The very telephone of *JR*.

The loss of character reaches its logical end for Mr. Palomar when he decides, since he has had only a negligible influence on anyone or thing, without even altering his habits to "consider himself dead quite severely...."[79] After all, hadn't the underground man concluded "any sort of consciousness is a disease."[80]

The Reader

Gore Vidal reminds us there can be no great novels if there are no great readers. While Henry James' dramatic efforts were bombing down the street, Oscar Wilde, then the toast of the town, found it easier to be witty about the audience of his age "which reads so much it has no time to admire and writes so much it has no time to think."[1] But here we are in an age which features authors who write so much on the computer they don't have time to think and audiences who read very little or read badly. (If you watch an American film – with the exception of Woody Allen – in contrast to one by a European, you will never see bookshelves unless the *mise-en-scène* is a college or library.)

Ray Bradbury's *Fahrenheit 451* is already seriously out of date. We recall that a small number of choice people have been assigned literary works which they must memorize before the world burns them. But no one has to memorize anymore and no one need burn (except CD's). Audio recordings and TV and film and computers and movies – Dickens, Austen, and James, an irony for the last named, abysmal theatrical failure that he was – have changed everything, taking us back, in an unforeseen way, to epic times when stories were heard, not read. This does not, however, compromise the persistent power of the reader-listener, confirmed every day as we see walkers and runners plugged into earphones.

We might cite Don Quixote as the quintessential bad reader: "one must actually touch with his hands what appears to the eye if he is to avoid being deceived."[2] Emma Bovary is a bad reader as well, but unlike the Don's reading, which ultimately serves the world, Emma's is simply self-directed and destructive. Calvino's Lotaria, Ludmilla's sister, the perfect academic reader for whom so many of the game novels are written, reads with no concern for the intent of the author, and comes to books with her own theories. This elite interpreter, in contrast to the Dickensian middle class readership, does not spell the end of novels; it signals the end of the novel of moral seriousness. Poor Ludmilla simply wants to read, but Lotaria, who has lost the irony so necessary for good reading, agrees with those who impose on the text "the sublimation of repression," the "transgression of roles," "the sexual semantic codes," "the metalanguages of the body," the "polymorphic-perverse sexuality," "the homologies of the signifying structures," "production methods," "the laws of a market economy," "the processes of reification."[3] (Keep in mind a past exhibition in the New York Public Library illustrating the transformation of books into "containers" and "conveyers of information.")[4]

If Don Quixote is the first middle-class novel, Cervantes is also the novelist who gives the reader equal standing with the other inhabitants of the House of Fiction. We can find many cases in literature of authors encouraging the reader to help with the narrative, though Harold Bloom takes a rather extreme modern view that Cervantes invented endless ways of disrupting his own narrative to compel the reader to tell the story in place of the wary author.[5] When he came to the chapter on the Cave of Montesinos, the translator found in the margin Hamete's own handwriting confessing that though he believed everything up to a certain point, he could not accept this as a true story. On the other hand, how could he doubt the word of "the truest gentleman and knight of his age." Furthermore, how could Don Quixote fabricate, with such expedition, so detailed "a farrago of nonsense." Just one solution appeals to him. "You, wise reader, may decide for yourself, for I cannot, nor am I obliged, to do any more. I am only obliged to tell you that it is reported he confessed he invented the incident at the end of his life."[6]

In Diderot's *Jacques le fataliste*, the reader and the author seem to be on the same level. His narrator sasses his reader and invites him to sass back, to look for other meanings. The only rule he cares about is that once the reader allows him to begin a story, he "commits himself to hearing it through to the end," unless he himself breaks off. Then the reader can finish the story from that point on. If Jacques and his master come back together again, maybe you would like to go back to them, or would you stay with me. And, Reader, don't treat me like an automaton. Tell the story or not, I have to follow your wishes but also mine.[7] The one constant in these back and forth contradictory instructions is the interdependence of the narrator and the reader.

Even Kafka still acknowledges this mutual dependency, as it is weakening, between the artist and the audience in "Josephine the Singer, or The Mouse Folk." But in a book like *If on a winter's night a traveler*, which sees to it that reading becomes a frustrating experience by continually changing the books and the stories before they end, the reader is the determinant of the story through the marketplace. Fancy apparatuses are hooked up to a female who reads novels turned out continuously by a computer.[8] If attention is high, it goes commercial. If not, new combinations are tried. Just as Pirandello's characters came before the story, so here, ludicrously, the readers determine the very birth or death of the story.

And this is because the reader can no longer count on "a world completed."[9] Dickens of course composed two different endings for *Great Expectations* but no readers ever felt in reading Dickens' novels, (with the exception of *Edward Drood*), they were being offered an incomplete world. In a fragmented world, however, the author has no more dominion. We feel that John Fowles is made uncomfortable by conclusions as he changes around the plot and provides three alternative endings in *The French Lieutenant's Woman* of 1969, a choice which has become old hat in films, though polling the audience for an ending rings a change.

The new frontier, Tim Parks writes, is the hypertext computer story, which puts readers in the driver's seat, choosing on their own a non-linear narrative, music, even images within a certain framework. This does away not only with the importance of the author (the reader chooses rather than submits) but the hope for any kind of communal interpretations. Take the case of Peter Molyneux, master video game deviser, who is interested not only in what kind of story a player makes up, but what kind of person he was when he played it. Molyneux's specialty is "god games," where, in a game called "Fable," for instance, the author-reader as player "often acts as a virtual god and the player's presence is known by the virtual characters inside his games." The player can make the decision to be good or evil, to be feared, worshipped, loved. The one effect the inventor hopes it will have, which we find more subtly in the Bildungsroman, is that it will teach the player what kind of person he is.[10]

Disillusioned with films, Peter Greenaway is moving on to possibilities with the internet and other technologies which no longer feature linear narratives. Given the nature of his films, Matthew Mirapaul observes, which offer no extended stories but "archives of rich visual data that prompt viewers to leap from idea to idea," he is comfortable with digital technologies which would free him from the confines of old narrative demands. It is a modern irony that precisely because there can be no community, the single reader has no final control or authority over the story. He plans to give his film "The Moab Story" a web site featuring the protagonist Tulse Luper, which may continue into TV, computer games etc. Web site visitors will be invited to contribute their part or interpretations of a story. Readers will only be able to solve a puzzle or mystery by pooling their information, as each has a different set of clues. The highest-ranking contestant would have a chance to become a character in a future Luper film.[11]

Literary theory for a long time now has given the reader center stage, but who could have imagined reception theory would end up like this! The readers rule even what they have not yet read. Calvino's Ludmilla is always reading another book besides the one before her eyes, a book that does not yet exist, but which, since she wants it, cannot fail to exist. "Reading is going toward something that is about to be, and no one yet knows what it will be...," she says.[12] It is the reader who writes the book the author was not able to write. "The universe will express itself as long as somebody will be able to say, I read, therefore it writes,"[13] observes Calvino's Silas Flannery in his Diary. It is the reader who tells the tale. How far we have come from Henry James, whose thicket of prose in his magnificent prefaces bespeaks a "solicitude" for the reader as he piles "brick upon brick."[14]

The author of the game novel may be more intelligent than the text but the reader is more intelligent than the author or the text. Mutual interaction will not work anymore. A reader in our technological age has no use for a creator since he himself is the author and can choose any of a number of turns for the non-linear plot, (eliminating immediately any choices grimly or otherwise narrowed), any number of characters who can change their identities, (cartoons though they be), and their lives (shallow as they are).

Hypertext allows the user to find a number of different results, and every reader's experience will be different. As we are constructing our plots, the characters by necessity become cardboard figures which can be moved about at will, from one plot to the other, one scene, one adventure. The narrative, if such we can call a non-linear experimentation, is better off without endings. The reader decides when he is finished reading and simply clicks the computer off. As for stories, movies and television have been the chief purveyors, and even they are entering the age of games, with multiple interpretations and, no irony intended, "animated" characters.

In such a non-resistant atmosphere, how can we hope to have a community of readers, (the bloggers in chat rooms are no substitute, nor are audiences for film or a TV series, though they probably come closest to the old communal experience). The printed word promoting individualism but, at the same time, creating great communities of readers culminating in Victorian frenzies of new installment expectations, has lost its power. (Exceptions may be made, I suppose, for runs like the Harry Potter craze). You could be Calvino's reader in *If on a winter's night a traveler* "impatient to get in touch with the Other Reader, to ask her if her copy is like yours, to tell her your conjecture, the information you have gathered… I'm not actually sure even of the title or the author's name."[15] That means, of course, that you will not be reading the same books. At the end of his novel, Reader and Reader, man and wife, lie in "a great double bed," receiving "your parallel readings." Each is off on his/her own journey, Ludmilla with her book, her husband with *If on a winter's night a traveler*; both lead, we now know, through a maze of disappearing texts.

The novelist Morelli in *Hopscotch* suggests that the reader should become obliged to be an accomplice as the text "whispers to him underneath the conventional exposition other more esoteric directions."[16]

And how shall we readers be accomplices? Well, Horacio sums up Morelli's case. "What good is a writer if he can't destroy literature?... And what good are we if we don't help as much as we can in that destruction."17

So this is what we have come to. Nabokov's Kimbote may be fatuous and quite mad, but, in the end, he speaks truth to his students: "What if we awake one day, all of us, and find ourselves utterly unable to read? I wish you to gasp not only at what you read but at the miracle of its being readable." Yet he himself is in a novel of game which is determined not to give us a readable universe – that universe we took for granted on summer afternoons, beautiful words indeed, buried deep in a wonderful story.

Abbreviations

IF – *If on a winter's night a traveler,* Calvino

DQ – *The Ingenious Gentleman Don Quixote de la Mancha* , Cervantes, Putnam edition

JF – *Jacques the Fatalist,* Diderot

JA – *Joseph Andrews,* Fielding

IL – *The Iliad*

OD – *The Odyssey*

LTC – *Love in the Time of Cholera,* Gabriel García Márquez

TS – *Tristram Shandy,* Sterne

T – *The Peloponnesian War,* The Landmark Thucydides

AEN – *The Aeneid*

NOTES

Preface
1. Lukács, *The Theory of the Novel*, 56.
2. See Nietzsche, "Twilight of the Idols" in *The Portable Nietzsche*, 515–16.

Thoughts from an Epic Prison

The Oldest and Newest Story
1. Lukács, *The Theory of the Novel*, 80.
2. Wilde, "Intentions" in *The Artist as Critic*, 307.
3. T, 5.26.421.
4. Ibid., 1.22.4.
5. Hanson, *A War Like No Other*, 82.
6. TS, Howard Anderson on 614.
7. Nietzsche , "The Birth of Tragedy" in the *Portable Nietzsche*, 91.

La Ronde
1. quoted in Weil, "*The Iliad*, Poem of Might" in *Simone Weil Reader*, 168.
2. T, 1.143, 432/1.
3. See William James, *The Meaning of Truth*, 238, *Pragmatism*, 68, "A World of Pure Experience" in *A Pluralistic Universe and Essays*, 1161, *The Principles of Psychology*, vol. 1, 245-6, *Essays in Radical Empiricism* , 45.
4. IL, Bk.1, 366, AEN, Bk.9, 279-281.
5. See Plutarch, 198.
6. T, 2.31.431, T −2.56.430.
7. Ibid., 2.67.430.
8. Ibid., 7.29.413.

9. Hanson, *A War Like No Other*, 106 and see T, 3.25-50 for background.
10. T, 4:24. 425.
11. Ibid., 8.31.412/1, 8.41.412/1.
12. IL, Bk.6, 143.
13. Ibid., Bk.6, 143.
14. *Beowulf*, 155.
15. T, 5.88.416.
16. Ibid., 5.116.416/5.
17. Ibid., 2.92.429, 4.43.425.
18. IL, Bk.15, 354.
19. T, 2.42.431/0.
20. AEN, Bk.10, 321.
21. *Beowulf*, 97.
22. Calvino, *The Nonexistent Knight*, 18-19.
23. T, 416-6.94.414, T – 7.34.413.
24. Ibid., 7.40.413, IL – Bk.9, 218, OD, Bk.16, 305.
25. Joyce, *Ulysses*, 141.
26. T. 7.82 – 83 – 84 – 85 –86 - 87.413.
27. Zeitlin, 24.
28. T, 8.87.411.

And Death Shall Have No Distinction

1. IL, Bk.8, 183.
2. Wilde, "The Decay of Lying" in *The Artist as Critic*, 291.
3. See Lukács, *The Theory of the Novel*, 64 for nature is adequate.
4. T, 3.111.426/5.
5. Ibid., 1.50.433.
6. Hanson, *A War Like No Other*, 143-4, 183-4.
7. T, 453, 7.44.413.
8. IL, Bk.6, 143.
9. Adorno, "On Epic Naiveté" in *Notes to Literature*, vol. 1, 25.
10. OD, Fitzgerald's Afterword, 493.
11. IL, Bk.21, 499, Bk.13, 319, Bk.16, 399, Bk.16, 388, Bk.14, 345, Bk.13, 305.
12. AEN , Bk.10, 307.
13. Weil, 154.
14. IL, Bk.23, 557.
15. Ibid., Bk.7, 175.
16. AEN, Bk.11, 339.
17. McEwan, *Atonement*, 299.

18. AEN, Bk.10, 324
19. DQ, 342.

The Myth of Progress

1. T, 4.95.424/3, Oenophyta with Myronides, T, 2.36.431/o, enlarged empire.
2. Hanson, *A War Like No Other*, 131.
3. T, 1.74 and 5.432, saviors of the Helenic world.
4. Ibid., 1.144.432/1.
5. AEN, Bk.1, 20.
6. Ibid., Bk.1, 26.
7. DQ, 972.
8. T, 2.43.431/o.
9. IL, Bk.9, 156.
10. Ibid., Bk.24, 592.
11. AEN, Bk.12, 383.
12. OD, Bk.16, 297.
13. T, 2.61.430.

Reading the Heroic Story Poorly

1. T, 2.41.431/o.
2. See Kagan, *Pericles of Athens and the Birth of Democracy*, 137-8.
3. See Lukács, *The Theory of the Novel*, 89 for inner security of hero.
4. T, 2.35.431/o.
5. Ibid., 2.38.431/o ff
6. IL, Bk.23, 555.
7 Ortega, "Signs of the Times" in *The Modern Theme*, 84.
8. T, 2.64.430, unrivaled, T, 2.40.431/o ff, power of Athens.
9. Ibid., 2.64.430.
10. Ibid., T, 2.64.430.
11. Ibid., 2.40.431/o.
12. Kagan, *Pericles of Athens and the Birth of Democracy*, 169-71.
13. Plutarch, 195.
14. Nietzsche, "Beyond Good and Evil", 39.
15. T, 2.64.430.
16. See Plutarch, 188.
17. T, 2:43.431/o.
18. Ibid., 4.59.424.
19. Ibid., 2.39.431/o, and 2.40.431/o.
20. Ibid., 6.8.415 ff and IL, Bk. 18, 445.
21. T, 2.54.430.

22. Ibid., 7.50.413.
23. Euripides, "The Trojan Women" in *The Complete Greek Tragedies*, 630.
24. T, 7.75.413.
25. Ibid., 3.82.427.
26. Ibid., 1.42.433.
27. Aristophanes, "Lysistrata" in *Lysistrata/ The Acharnians/ The Clouds*, 228.
28. T, 1.141.432/1.
29. Ibid., 2.64.430 – Pericles' last oration.
30. Ibid., 2.41.431/0.
31. Ibid., 2.63.430.
32. Ibid., 4.87.424.
33. Ibid., 2.43.431/0 ff – Pericles' funeral oration.
34. Euripides, "The Trojan Women", 624.
35. OD, Bk.13, 239.
36. AEN, Bk.2, 33 ff.
37. DQ, 703.
38. T, 2.65.430.
39. Plutarch, 205 and 246, the Megarian Decree.
40. Euripides, "The Acharnians", 72.
41. T, 2.40.431/0 for example.
42. Ibid., 1.22.
43. Ibid., 2.37.431/0.
44. Ibid., 2.41.431/0.
45. Ibid., 2.39.431/0 ff.
46. Ibid., 40,1.70.432.
47. IL, Bk.13, 318-19.
48. T, 6.18.415.
49. Ibid., 2.41.431/0.
50. Ibid., 2.62,430.
51. Ibid., 4.34.425.
52. Zeitlin, 74.
53. T, 4.84.424.
54. Ibid., 4.105.424/3.
55. Ibid., 5.105.416.
56. Ibid., 5.99.416 ff.
57. Ibid., 2.89.429, 2.90.429.
58. Ibid., 7.66.413 ff.
59. Ibid., 4.108.424/3
60. Ibid., 5.103.416.
61. Hanson, *A War Like No Other*, 103, throwing prisoners live into a pit, Kagan,

Pericles of Athens and the Birth of Democracy, 30, "disabled and wounded".
62. T, 1.79.432
63. Ibid., 1.118. 432.
64. Ibid., 4.19.425ff, 4.21.425.
65. Hanson, 277-8, *A War Like No Other*, Sparta playing defense.
66. See T, 4.27.425.
67. Ibid., 5.115.416
68. Aristophanes, "Lysistrata", ftnotes 250.
69. Ibid., 231.
70. T, 5.18.422/1 ff.
71. Ibid., 6.1.416/5.
72. Ibid., 8.96.411.
73. Aristophanes, "The Acharnians", 44-5)

The Public Epic

1. Finley, *Four Stages of Greek Thought*, 7.
2. IL, Bk.12, 290-291.
3. T, 3.82.427.
4. Ibid., 3.82.427.
5. Ibid., 2.39.431/o.
6. Ibid., 2.40.431/o.
7. See Hanson, *A War Like No Other*, 45 for "rural refugees.
8. T, 2.42.431/o, fighting in the country's battles, T, 2:43.431/o, the offering of the lives.
9. Ibid., 2.44.431/o, fortunate indeed..., 2.43.431/o, Think of the wonderful stories....
10. OD, Bk.8, 141-2.
11. AEN , Bk.9, 275-6.
12. T, 2.45.431/o.
13. "The Trojan Women", 654
14. AEN, Bk.11, 337.
15. T, 2.43.431/o.
16. Weil, "*The Iliad*, Poem of Might", 178.
17. IL, Bk.4, 89.
18. Ibid., Bk.18, 444.
19. Plutarch, 211.
20. Aristophanes, "Lysistrata", 184, 207.
21. Aeschylus, "Agamemnon", 48.
22. See Kagan, *Pericles of Athens and the Birth of Democracy*, 115, 117.
23. T, 1.120.432/1.

24. Ibid., 6.18.415.
25. Aristophanes, "The Acharnians", 54.
26. Ibid., 97 and 98.
27. Aristophanes, "Lysistrata", 201.
28. T, 1.45.431/0.
29. OD, Bk.8, 142.
30. Euripides, "The Trojan Women", 657.
31. IL, Bk.18, 446.
32. AEN, Bk.9, 277, Euryalus has someone else tell his mother he is going into battle.
33. IL, Bk.6, 144.
34. Kagan, *Pericles of Athens and the Birth of Democracy*, 68.
35. AEN, Bk.1, 4-5.
36. see Weil, 154 for "far-off world".
37. IL, Bk.19, 467.
38. Ibid., Bk.21, 499.
39. Ibid., Bk.14, 345, father and mother mourn, , Bk. 5, 114, will never welcome them home..., Bk 5, 114, "with kites for company"..., Bk.11, 263, "for from Larisa's rich"..., Bk.17, 416, Bk.20, 485, "terror of all soldiers".
40. AEN, Bk.10, 314.
41. IL, Bk.11, 258.
42. Ibid., Bk.24, 592.
43. AEN , Bk.11, 339.
44. OD, Bk.24, 446-7.
45. IL, Bk.2, 50.
46. OD, Bk.6, 104, Bk. 13, 230.
47. Ibid, Bk.22, 418.
48. Ibid., Bk.23, 430.
49. TS, 256.
50. OD, Bk.23, 440, Bk.24, 459-60.
51. Ibid., Bk.11, 189.
52. LTC, 211.
53. AEN, Bk.6, 182-3.
54. Ibid., Bk.1, 18-19, 22, magistrates and senate etc., Bk.4, 103 ff, law's dominion.
55. Ibid., Bk.3, 70-71, new-found hearths, Bk.5, 152, boundaries, laws and assemblies, Bk.5, 147, "a town and home"....
56. Ibid., Bk.8, 251, near the cold stream, Bk.8, 240, "Marveling...", see also 230.

An Epic Loss of Will

1. AEN, Bk. 1, 12-13.
2. IL, Bk.19, 469-70, "Why prophesy...", Bk.1, 23, "Why tell you what you know".

3. Ibid., Bk.15, 351.
4. OD, Bk.6, 105, Bk.23, 434, Bk.18, 342.
5. Lukács, 63, 88.
6. Ortega, *Meditations on Quixote*, 148-9.
7. IL, Bk.16, 398.
8. Ibid., Bk.17, 413.
9. Ibid., Bk.19, 463.
10. Ibid., Bk.15, 358.
11. Ibid., Bk.5, 130.
12. Ibid., Bk.15, 523.
13. JA, 151.
14. IL, Bk.17, 411-12.
15. Ibid., Bk.17, 425.
16. Ibid., Bk.22, 517.
17. *Beowulf*, 207.
18. IL, Bk.20, 476.
19. OD, Bk.5, 93, Bk.13, 242.
20. Ibid., Bk.20, 376.
21. AEN, Bk.3, 81-2.
22. IL, Bk.5, 111-12-13 and Bk.23, 559.
23. Ibid., Bk.17, 427.
24. *Beowulf*, 71 and 39.
25. IL, Bk.16, 393, Bk. 15, 350.
26. AEN , Bk.5, 153.
27. IL, Bk.5, 121.
28. OD, Bk.6, 100.
29. IL, Bk.5, 123.
30. Ibid., Bk.20, 477-8.
31. Ibid., Bk,11, 253-4, Bk.17, 421.
32. Ibid., Bk.6, 141.
33. AEN, Bk.11, 340.
34. AEN, Bk.8, 234.
35. *Beowulf*, 155.
36. Kagan, *Pericles of Athens and the Birth of Democracy*, 186.
37. T, 1.78.432.
38. T, 5.108.416.
39. AEN, Bk.4, 108.
40. See Santayana, *Interpretations of Poetry and Religion*, 45.
41. IL, Bk.19, 459.
42. Ibid., Bk.19, 465.

43. Ibid., Bk.19, 460.
44. AEN, Bk.3, 65.
45. IL, Bk.3, 73.
46. AEN Bk.1, 25.
47. OD, Bk.1, 2.
48. IL, Bk.5, 128.
49. T, 8.1.413, "angry with the orators", see Hanson, 84, more powerful since the plague.
50. OD , Bk.3, 41-2.
51. AEN , Bk.9, 262-263.
52. See Hamilton, *The Greek Way*, 212.
53. AEN , Bk.2, 57.
54. OD Bk.9, 161.
55. AEN, Bk.12, 385-6.
56. Ibid., Bk.8, 234.
57. Ibid., Bk.8, 236.
58. Ibid., Bk.1, 28.
59. See Hamilton, *The Roman Way*, 115.
60. AEN, Bk.8, 230.
61. Ibid., Bk.2, 58.
62. Ibid., Bk.3, 80.
63. Ibid., Bk.9, 269.

An Epic Failure of Empathic Imagination

1. IL, Bk.21, 496-7.
2. Tolstoy, "Ivan Ilyich", 250.
3. IL, Bk.24, 585.
4. See Lukács, *The Theory of the Novel*, 71, 85, 123.
5. Aeschylus, "Agamemnon", 90
6. AEN, Bk.1, 26.
7. OD, Bk.11, 197.
8. IL, Bk.14, 332.
9. See Finley, *Four Stages of Greek Thought*, 26.
10 Dante, *The Inferno*, Canto 26.
11. See Gordon, *Imagining the End of Life in Post-Enlightenment Poetry – Voices against the Void*, 52-3, Tennyson's "Ulysses".
12. End of *A Portrait of the Artist as a Young Man*.
13. Lukács, *The Theory of the Novel*, 30.
14. OD, Bk.11, 201.
15. Ibid., Bk.11, 201.

16. IL, Bk.21, 497.
17. Ibid., Bk.24, 576.
18. Ibid., Bk.22, 517.
19. OD, Bk.8, 141.
20. Ibid., Bk.9, 146.
21. IL, Bk.22, 518-19.
22. Ibid., Bk.18, 439.
23. Ibid., Bk.18, 439.
24. Ibid., Bk.19, 463.
25. Ibid., Bk.24, 572.
26. Ibid., Bk.22, 527.
27. Ibid., Bk.22, 526.
28. Ibid., Bk.24, 584.
29. Ibid., Bk.24, 586.
30. Ibid., Bk.24, 584-5.
31. Ibid., Bk.24, 586.
32. Ibid., Bk.22, 527.
33. Ibid., Bk.22, 568.
34. Ibid., Bk.24, 588.

Sanity and Slaughter

1. IL, Bk.6, 146.
2. T, 2.7.431.
3. Ibid., 6.9.418 ff.
4. Ibid, 6.26.415.
5. Calvino, *The Nonexistent Knight*, 44.
6. T, 6.24.415 ff.
7. Ibid., 472-6.75.413.
8. *New York Times Book Review*, Aug 25, 2002, Eugen Weber reviews *The Road to Verdun* by Ian Ousby, and see Fussell, 12 and 13.
9. Fussell, *The Great War and Modern Memory*, 10.
10. IL, Bk.3, 71.
11. Ibid., Bk.7, 170-1.
12. Ibid., Bk.6, 148-9, Bk.6, 149.
13. Ibid., Bk.12, 291.
14. Cavell, "The Fact of Television" in *Themes out of School*, 166-7.
15. Lukács, *The Theory of the Novel*, 80.

How the Novel Got Its Game

The House of Fiction
1. DQ, 31.
2. JA, xiv, JA, 197, TS, 22.
3. TS, 11 and 15.
4. IF, 92.
5. Kundera, *The Art of the Novel*, 83.
6. TS, 7.
7. JA, 67.
8. See Robbe-Grillet, *For a New Novel*, 10.
9. Dinesen, "The Cardinal's First Tale" in *Last Tales*, 6.
10. JA, 3, Unamuno, *Tragic Sense of Life*, 325.
11. DQ, 939.
12. Ibid., 878.
13. Ibid., 557-60, 527.
14. Lukács, *The Theory of the Novel*, 123.
15. Dostoevsky, "Notes from the Underground", 295.
16. McEwan, *Atonement*, 87.
17. Benjamin, "The Storyteller" in *Illuminations*, 101.
18. Lukács, *The Theory of the Novel*, 112.
19. Auden cited in Trilling, "On the Teaching of Modern Literature" in *The Moral Obligation to be Intelligent*, 385.
20. Foucault, cited in the Norton edition of *Don Quijote*, edited by Diana de Armas Wilson, 793.
21. "Notes from the Underground", 377, 323.
22. JA, 205.
23. Trilling, "The America of John Dos Passos" in *The Moral Obligation to be Intelligent*, 9.
24. Cortázar, *Hopscotch*, 164.
25. Ortega, "Signs of the Times" in *The Modern Theme*, 81-2-3.
26. Svevo, *Confessions of Zeno*, 144.
27. Wordsworth - Supplementary to "Preface of 1815 Lyrical Ballads".
28. TS, 276.
29. DQ, 914, 726.
30. Mistry, *A Fine Balance*, 377.
31. DQ, 262-3.
32. Ibid., 825.
33. TS, 298.

34. Ibid., 38.
35. Joyce, *Ulysses*, 333.
36. LTC, 108.
37. Lukács, 56.
38. Franzen, *How to Be Alone*, 178.
39. Foer, *Everything Is Illuminated*, 247.
40. Sebald, *Austerlitz*, 205.
41. See Norton edition of *Don Quijote* – xi, Diana de Armas, *La Galatea* and DQ, 57, and see Chapters II and III of Part 2 of DQ for conversation with Carrasco etc.
42. Foucault, cited in Norton edition of *Don Quijote*, 794.
43. IF, 43.

Form as a Problem

1. Carlos Fuentes in Norton edition of *Don Quijote*, 778 quoting Claudio Guillen.
2. Joyce, *Ulysses*, 506.
3. Cortázar, *Hopscotch*, 396.
4. DQ, 459, 116, 95.
5. TS, 37, 52
6. Lawrence, "Whitman" in *Studies in Classic American Literature*, 184.
7. first line of "The Dry Salvages" by T.S. Eliot, Trilling, "Huckleberry Finn" in *The Moral Obligation to Be Intelligent*, 139.
8. LTC, 168.
9. Ibid., 293.
10. DQ, 782.
11. Ibid., 523, 160.
12. Ibid., 80-81.
13. JA, 218, 11.
14. Ibid., 31.
15. JA, 51, 48.
16. DQ, 80-81.
17. Ibid., 953.
18. Ibid., 861.
19. DQ, 697, 790 and TS, 401.
20. TS, 82.
21. DQ, 581, 161, 736.
22. Joyce, *Ulysses*, 280.
23. Joyce, *A Portrait of the Artist as a Young Man*, 175.
24. Lukács, 104, 175.
25. Calvino, *Mr. Palomar*, 105-6.
26. Ibid., 116-17.

27. Lawrence, "The Novel" in *Reflections on the Death of a Porcupine and Other Essays*, 16.
28. LTC, 345.
29. Sebald, *Austerlitz*, 265.
30. Cortázar, *Hopscotch*, 7.
31. Kundera, 17 and see Lukács.
32. Dinesen's Cardinal in "The Cardinal's First Tale", see later reference.
33. Adorno – "The Position of the Narrator in the Contemporary Novel", 32.
34. Joyce, *Ulysses*, 273.
35. Ibid., 83.
36. LTC, 13, 17, 108.
37. Calvino, *Invisible Cities*, 28-9.
38. Ibid., 138.
39. Ibid., 128.
40. T. S. Eliot, "Little Gidding", *Four Quartets*.
41. IF, 14.
42. JA, 20.
43. Joyce, *A Portrait of the Artist as a Young Man*, 11-12.
44. LTC, 16.
45. IF, 8.
46. Trilling, "Art, Will, and Necessity" in *The Moral Obligation to Be Intelligent*, 521.
47. Kundera, 42.
48. Calvino, *Mr. Palomar*, 4.
49. Calvino, *Invisible Cities*, 112-13.

Morality as a Problem

1. Henry James contrasts "memorized morality" to his father's morality in his memoirs.
2. Diderot, *Rameau's Nephew*, 50.
3. Nietzsche, "Twilight of the Idols", 515-16.
4. Joyce, *Ulysses*, 4, 169.
5. Kundera, 102-3.
6. Svevo, *Confessions of Zeno*, 368, 299.
7. Calvino, *The Cloven Viscount*, 243.
8. Calvino, *Cosmicomiche*, 127, 134, 135-7.
9. DQ, 405.
10. Ibid., 893.
11. *Bleak House*, 188.
12. Calvino, *The Cloven Viscount*, 246.
13. Calvino, *Mr. Palomar*, 61.

14. Sebald, *Austerlitz*, 136.
15. Nabokov, *Pale Fire*, Introduction by Richard Rorty.
16. LTC, 223-4, 43.
17. Ibid., 263, 321, 345.
18. García Marquez, *One Hundred Years of Solitude*, 450 and 456.
19. Kundera, 15-16, and see "Sterne's Great Game" by John Bayley, *New York Review of Books*, Oct.24, 2002.
20. TS, see Richard Lanham, 593.
21. Ibid., 72.
22. Ibid., 72.
23. Barzun, 7.
24. Calvino, *Mr. Palomar*, 55.
25. Robbe-Grillet, 86-7.
26. Calvino, *Cosmicomiche*, 88-9, 38-9.
27. Wilde, "Intentions" in *The Artist as Critic*, 293.
28. Bayley, "The Order of Battle at Trafalgar" in *The Order of Battle at Trafalgar and Other Essays*, 11.
29. Calvino, *Mr. Palomar*, 126.
30. McEwan, *Atonement*, 265.

The Truth of the Story

1. Dinesen, "The Cardinal's First Tale", 24.
2. OD, Bk.9, 145.
3. *Beowulf*, 143-4.
4. DQ, 200, 408.
5. Ibid., 264.
6. JF, 214.
7. Ibid., 30.
8. TS, 410.
9. Calvino, *The Baron in the Trees*, 123.
10. Svevo, *Confessions of Zeno*, 75.
11. IF, 220.
12. Ibid., 109.
13. Foer, *Everything Is Illuminated*, 180.
14. DQ, 45.
15. Ibid., 155.
16. Ibid., 528.
17. Ibid., 895, 896, 898, 974-5.
18. Ibid., 897-8.
19. Dinesen, "The Immortal Story" in *Anecdotes of Destiny and Ehrengard*, 185.

20. Coetzee, *Slow Man*, 117, 159.
21. Ibid., 228-9, 232-3.
22. IF, 92.
23. JF, 22.
24. McEwan, *Atonement*, 142.

The Author

1. Cather, *The Song of the Lark*, 44.
2. JA, 353, 221, 56.
3. TS, 6.
4. Ibid., 10, 40-42, 60, 6-7, 237.
5. JF, 222.
6, TS, 57.
7. JF, 59, 222.
8. Ibid., 200.
9. See "Notes from the Underground", 263.
10. TS, 311.
11. Ibid., 332, 207.
12. JF, 227.
13. Ibid., 166.
14. Ibid., 21.
15. See Diana de Armas Wilson, editor of *Don Quijote*, xi.
16. DQ, 11, 31-2, 70.
17. Ibid., 557.
18. Ibid., 555, 687.
19. Ibid., 764.
20. Ibid., 912.
21. Ibid., 538, 964.
22. Svevo, *Confessions of Zeno*, 68.
23. JA, 274.
24. Howe, *Thomas Hardy*, 110-11.
25. Joyce, *Ulysses*, 318.
26. Henry James, "The Lesson of Balzac" in *The Future of the Novel*, 117.
27. JA, 27.
28. OD, Bk.13, 239.
29. AEN, Bk.8, 234, Lawrence, "The Spirit of Place" in *Studies in Classic American Literature*, 13.
30. JF, 165.
31. TS, 446-7.
32. McEwan, *Atonement*, 38.

33. Ibid., 156.
34. IF, 155.
35. Nabokov, *Pale Fire*, 87.
36. Ibid., 244.
37. Ibid., 27.
38. Ibid., 28-9.
39. Pirandello, "Six characters in search of an author", xxix.
40. See Kundera, 158.
41. Lawrence, "Whitman" in *Studies in Classic American Literature*, 183-4, "The Novel" in *Death of a Porcupine and Other Essays*, 104, 108.
42. TS, 222, 307.
43. Sebald, *Austerlitz*, 119.
44. Cortázar, *Hopscotch*, 443, 556.
45. *Notes from the Underground*, 294, 376.
46. IF, 178-9.
47. TS, 292.
48. Calvino, *The Nonexistent Knight*, 106, 140.
49. Quoted in a review of *Coming Soon!!!* called "The End of the Road" by Jennifer Schuessler, *The New York Times*, Nov. 4, 2001.
50. Hazlitt, 28.
51. IF, 180-1.
52. Quoted in Introduction by Susan Sontag in *A Barthes Reader*.

The Characters

1. Dinesen, "The Cardinal's First Tale", 24.
2. Thomas Mann, *Joseph the Provider*, trans. H. T. Lowe Porter, New York, Alfred A. Knopf, 350.
3. Dinesen, "The Cardinal's First Tale", 24.
4. Benjamin, "The Storyteller" in *Illuminations*, 102.
5. Marcus, *Dickens from Pickwick to Dombey*, 86-7.
6. Dinesen, "The Cardinal's First Tale", 25-6.
7. See Marcus – 78.
8. DQ, 972.
9. Ortega, *Meditations on Quixote*, 148-9.
10. DQ, 211.
11. Ibid., 978.
12. Ibid., 531.
13. Svevo, *Confessions of Zeno*, 368, 372.
14. DQ, 138.
15. Ortega, *Meditations on Quixote*, 37.
16. TS, 298.

17. Quoted in Ibid., 489, 548.
18. DQ, 737.
19. TS, 256.
20. Ibid., 81.
21. Ibid., 429.
22. Joyce, *Ulysses*, 140, 133, 148 -149, 643.
23. Ibid., 202.
24. DQ, 546.
25. LTC, 323.
26. DQ, 987, 546, 535.
27. Coetzee, *Slow Man*, 200.
28. Pirandello, 13.
29. Ibid., 61.
30. Ibid., 61.
31. See William James, "A Pluralistic Universe and Essays" in *William James – Writings 1902 - 1910* , 651.
32. Pirandello, 61, 63.
33. TS, 140.
34. Agnon, *Shira*, 423, 254.
35. Pirandello, 62.
36. McEwan, *Atonement*, 153.
37. "Notes from the Underground", 376, 305.
38. Ibid., 265-6, 277-8.
39. Bloom, *How to Read and Why*, 195.
40, Dinesen, "The Cardinal's First Tale, 25- 6.
41. DQ, 49.
42. Ibid., 709.
43. Ibid.,776-8.
44. Aristotle's *Poetics*, 643, item 15.
45. Barzun, 785.
46. "Notes from the Underground", 268.
47. Cortázar, *Hopscotch*, 340.
48. IF, 37-8.
49. *Austerlitz*, 31.
50. Calvino, *Mr. Palomar*, 65.
51. IF, 15.
52. Pirandello, 9, see Finley, 95.
53. Sebald, *Austerlitz*, 158-9.
54. Calvino, *Mr. Palomar*, 113-14.
55. Ibid., 118.

56. "Notes from the Underground", 266.
57. See Kundera, 24.
58. See Zadie Smith's "The Autograph Man" in *Radcliffe Quarterly*, Winter 2003, 24.
59. Lee Siegel, "Freud and His Discontents" in *The New York Times Book Review*, May 8, 2005.
60. Calvino, *The Cloven Viscount*, 234-5.
61. Ibid., 191-2, 245.
62. Ibid., 216-17.
63. Calvino, *Mr. Palomar*, 14, IF, 162-3.
64. Sebald, *Austerlitz*, 76-7, 293.
65. Svevo, *Confessions of Zeno*, 134.
66. Ibid., 37.
67. Ibid., 113, 110.
68. Schapiro, *Impressionism, Reflections and Perceptions*, 312, and conversation with Professor Shehira Davezac at Indiana University.
69. See Zadie Smith, "The Limited Circle is Pure" in *The New Republic*, Nov. 3, 2003.
70, Calvino, *Invisible Cities*, 48.
71. Ibid., 28.
72. Gaddis, *JR* , 172, 246-7.
73. Ibid., 335.
74. Calvino, *Mr. Palomar*, 25.
75. Cortázar, *Hopscotch*, 256, 455.
76. Calvino, *Mr. Palomar*, 104.
77. Ibid., 83.
78. IF, 11.
79. Calvino, *Mr. Palomar*, 121-3.
80. "Notes from the Underground", 267.

The Reader

1. Wilde, "To Read, or Not to Read" in *The Artist as Critic*, 28.
2. DQ, 576.
3. IF, 185, 75 and 91.
4. "Books as Art Objects - Reading Is Optional" in *The New York Times*, Friday, Jan 2, 2004.
5. Harold Bloom in the Norton edition of *Don Quijote*, 781.
6. DQ, 665-6.
7. JF, 74, 251, also see Introduction, 12.
8. IF, 127-8.

9. Robbe-Grillet, *For a New Novel*, 156.

10. Tim Parks, "Tales Told by the Computer" in *The New York Review of Books*, Oct. 24, 2002, and see Stephen Totilo, "Letting Gamers Play God, and Now Themselves" in *The New York Times – Circuits –* Thursday, Sept. 2, 2004.

11. See Matthew Mirapaul's "An Auteur Packs His Bags To Venture Onto the Web" in *The New York Times*, May 19, 2003.

12. IF, 72.

13. Ibid., Silas Flannery in his Diary, 176.

14. Henry James, Preface to *Portrait of a Lady*.

15. IF, 44.

16. Cortázar, *Hopscotch*, 396.

17. Ibid., 442.

Bibliography

Adorno, Theodor W., "On Epic Naiveté", "The Position of the Narrator in the Contemporary Novel", in *Notes to Literature*, vol. 1, translated by Shierry Weber Nicholsen, edited by Rolf Tiedemann, Columbia University Press, New York, 1991

Aeschylus, "Agamemnon" in *The Complete Greek Tragedies*, vol.1, edited and translated by David Greene and Richmond Lattimore, University of Chicago Press, 1953

Agnon, S. Y., *Shira*, translated by Zeva Shapiro, Afterword by Robert Alter, Syracuse University Press, 1989

Aristophanes, *Lysistrata/ The Acharnians/ The Clouds*, translated with an Introduction by Alan H. Sommerstein, Penguin Classics, Penguin Books, London and New York, 1973

Aristotle, *Aristotle's Poetics,* Introduction Richard McKeon, Modern Library, Random House, New York, 1947

Barthes, Roland, *A Barthes Reader,* edited by Susan Sontag, Harper Collins Canada Lmt., 1996

Barzun, Jacques, *From Dawn to Decadence, 1500 to the Present, 500 Years of Western Cultural Life*, HarperCollins Publishers, New York, 2000

Bayley, John, *The Order of Battle at Trafalgar and Other Essays,* Weidenfeld and Nicholson, New York, 1987

Beckett, Samuel, *End Game*, Grove Press Inc. New York, 1958

Benjamin, Walter, *Illuminations*, translated by Harry Zohn, edited with an Introduction by Hannah Arendt, Harcourt Brace and World Inc., New York, 1955

Blamires, Harry, *The New Bloomsday Book*, Routledge, London and New York, 1996

Bloom, Harold, *How to Read and Why*, Scribner, New York, London etc., 2000

Bradbury, Ray, *Fahrenheit 451*, A Del Ray Book, Ballantine Books, 1950, 1978

Calvino, Italo, *The Baron in the Trees,* translated by Archibald Colquhoun, A Harvest Book, Harcourt Brace, New York, 1959 – (BT)
―――― *Cosmicomiche*, translated by William Weaver, Harcourt Brace and Co., San Diego, New York, London, 1968
―――― *If on a winter's night a traveler,* translated by William Weaver, Harvest Book, Harcourt, Inc., San Diego, New York, London, 1981
―――― *Invisible Cities*, translated by William Weaver, Harcourt Brace and Co., San Diego, New York, London, 1974
―――― *Mr. Palomar*, translated by William Weaver, Harcourt Brace Jovanovich, San Diego, New York, London 1985
―――― *The Nonexistent Knight and The Cloven Viscount*, translated by Archibald Colquhoun, Harvest Book, Harcourt Brace and Co., San Diego, New York, London 1962

Cather, Willa, *The Song of the Lark*, Introduction by Sharon O'Brien, Signet Classic, 1991, USA)

Cavell, Stanely, *Themes Out of School*, North Point Press, San Francisco, 1984

Cervantes, Miguel de, *Don Quijote*, 2 vols., translated by Burton Raffel edited by Diana de Armas Wilson, W.W. Norton and Co., New York, London, 1999
―――― *The Ingenious Gentleman Don Quixote de la Mancha*, edited and translated by Samuel Putnam, 2 vols, Viking Press, New York, 1949

Coetzee, J. M., *Slow Man*, Viking, New York, 2005

Cortázar, Julio, *Hopscotch*, translated by Gregory Rabassa, Pantheon Books, New York, 1966

Dante Alighieri, *The Inferno* – Canto 26, translated by Mark Musa, Indiana University Press, Bloomington, 1971

Dickens, Charles, *Bleak House*, edited by George Ford and Sylvère Monod, W. W. Norton, New York, London, 1977

Diderot, Denis, *Jacques the Fatalist*, translated by Michael Henry, Introduction by Martin Hall, Penguin Classics, Harmondsworth, Middlesex, England and New York, 1986
—— *Rameau's Nephew and Other Works*, translated by Jacques Barzun and Ralph H. Bowen, Introduction by Ralph Bowen, Doubleday Anchor Book, Garden City, New York, 1956

Dinesen, Isak, "The Cardinal's First Tale" in *Last Tales*, Random House, New York 1957
—— "The Immortal Story" in *Anecdotes of Destiny and Ehrengard*, Vintage International – Random House, New York, 1993

Donoghue, Denis, *Ferocious Alphabets*, Columbia University Press, New York, 1984

Dostoevsky, Fyodor, "Notes from the Underground" in *Great Short Works*, translated by David Magarshack, Introduction by Ronald Hingley, A Perennial Classic of Harper and Row, Publishers, New York, 1968

Euripides, "The Trojan Women" in *The Complete Greek Tragedies*, edited by David Grene and Richmond Lattimore, translated by Richmond Lattimore, University of Chicago Press, Chicago 1955

Fielding, Henry, *Joseph Andrews*, Introduction by Howard Mumford Jones, The Modern Library, New York, 1950

Finley, John H. Jr., *Four Stages of Greek Thought*, Stanford University Press, Stanford, California, 1966

Foer, Jonathan Safran, *Everything is Illuminated*, Perennial Books, HarperCollins, New York, 2003

Franzen, Jonathan, *How to Be Alone*, Farrar, Straus and Giroux, New York, 2002

Fussell, Paul, *The Great War and Modern Memory*, Oxford University Press, London, Oxford, New York, 1979

Gaddis, William, *JR*, Penguin Books, Hamondsworth, Middlesex, England and New York, 1975 and 1985

Gordon, David J., *Imagining the End of Life in Post-Enlightenment Poetry – Voices against the Void*, University Press of Florida, Gainesville/Tallahassee/Tampa/Boca Raton, etc. 2005

Hamilton, Edith *The Greek Way to Western Civilization*, New American Library, New York, 1957
────── *The Roman Way to Western Civilization*, The New American Library, New York, 1957

Hanson, Victor Davis, *A War Like No Other: How the Athenians and Spartans Fought the Peloponnesian War*, Random House, New York, 2005

Hazlitt, William, *The Plain Speaker, The Key Essays*, Introduction by Tom Paulin, edited by Duncan Wu, Blackwell Publishers, Maldin, MA, 1998

Heaney, Seamus, *Beowulf*, Farrar, Straus and Giroux, New York, 2000 –

Homer, *The Iliad*, translated by Robert Fitzgerald, Anchor Books, Doubleday and Co. Inc., Garden City, New York, 1975 – (IL)
────── *The Odyssey*, translated and Postscript by Robert Fitzgerald, Anchor Books, Doubleday and Co. Inc., Garden City, New York, 1963

Howe, Irving, *Thomas Hardy*, Collier Books, New York, 1966

James, Henry, "The Lesson of Balzac" in *The Future of the Novel, Essays on the Art of Fiction,* – edited and Introduction by Leon Edel, Vintage Books, New York, 1956 – (FN)
────── Preface to *Portrait of a Lady*

James, William, *Essays in Radical Empiricism,* Peter Smith, Gloucester MA, 1967
────── "A Pluralistic Universe and Essays" in *William James – Writings 1902 – 1910*, Library of America – New York, 1987
────── *Pragmatism and The Meaning of Truth*, Introduction by A. J. Ayer, Harvard University Press, Cambridge, 1975

———— *The Principles of Psychology*, vol. 1, Dover Publications, Inc., New York, 1950

Joyce, James, *Ulysses*, edited by Hans Walter Gabler with Wolfhard Steppe and Claus Melchior, Preface by Richard Ellmann, Forward by Hans Walter Gabler, Afterward by Michael Groden, Vintage Books – Random House, New York, 1986
———— *A Portrait of the Artist as a Young Man*, Introduction by Herbert Gorman, The Modern Library Publishers, New York, 1928

Kagan, Donald, *Pericles of Athens and the Birth of Democray*, The Free Press – Macmillan, New York, 1991

Kundera, Milan, *The Art of the Novel*, translated by Linda Asher, Harper Perennial – HarperCollins, 2000

Lawrence, D. H., "The Novel" in *Reflections on the Death of a Porcupine and Other Essays*, A Midland Book of Indiana University Press, Bloomington IN and London, 1963
———— "The Spirit of Place", "Whitman" in *Studies in Classic American Literature*, Doubleday and Co. Inc., Garden City, New York, 1955

Lebowitz, Naomi, *The Philosophy of Literary Amateurism*, Missouri University Press, Columbia and London, 1994

Lukács, Georg, *The Theory of the Novel*, translated by Anna Bostock, M.I.T. Press, Cambridge MA, 1971

McEwan, Ian, *Atonement*, Nan A. Talese Book, Doubleday, New York, London, Toronto, Sydney Aukland, 2002

Marcus, Steven, *Dickens from Pickwick to Dombey*, Simon and Schuster, 1965, New York

Márquez, Gabriel García, *Love in the Time of Cholera*, translated by Edith Grossman, Penguin Books – Viking Penguin, New York, London, 1989
———— *One Hundred Years of Solitude*, translated by Gregory Rabassa, Perennial Classics, New York, 1998 – (One Hundred)

Mistry, Rohinton, *A Fine Balance*, Vintage International – Random House, New York, 1997

Nabokov, Vladimir, *The Defense*, Popular Library, New York, 1964
——— *Pale Fire*, Vintage International – Random House, New York, 1989
——— *Pale Fire*, Introduction by Richard Rorty, Everyman's Library, Alfred A. Knopf, New York, Toronto, 1992

Naipaul, V. S., *A House for Mister Biswas*, Alfred A. Knopf, New York, 1983

Nietzsche, Friedrich, "Twilight of the Gods", "The Birth of Tragedy", "Beyond Good and Evil" in *The Portable Nietzsche*, edited and translated by Walter Kaufmann, Penguin Books – Viking, Harmondsworth, Middlesex England, 1954

Ortega, Y Gasset, *Meditations on Quixote*, translated by Evelyn Rugg and Diego Marín, W. W. Norton and Co., New York, 1961
——— *The Modern Theme*, translated By James Cleugh, Introduction by Jose Ferrater Mora, Harper Torchbooks, Harper and Brothers, New York, 1961

Pirandello, Luigi, *Six characters in Search of an Author*, translated and Introduction by Eric Bentley, Signet Classic Book, Penguin, New York, Australia, Canada, New Zealand

Plutarch, *Plutarch's Lives*, Modern Library, New York, 1932

Postman, Neil, *Building a Bridge to the 18th c, How the Past Can Improve Our Future*, Vintage Books – Random House, New York, 1999

Rawson, Claude, *Satire and Sentiment 1660-1830*, Yale University Press, New Haven and London, 1994

Robbe-Grillet, Alain, *For a New Novel, Essays on Fiction*, translated by Richard Howard, Northwestern University Press, Evanston, Illinois 1989

Santayana, George, "Homeric Hymns" in *Interpretations of Poetry and Religion*, Harper and Brothers Publishers, New York, 1957

Schapiro, Meyer, *Impressionism, Reflections and Perceptions*, George Braziller, New York, 1997

Sebald, W. G., *Austerlitz*, translated by Anthea Bell, Random House, New York, 2001

Sennett, Richard, *The Fall of Public Man, On the Social Psychology of Capitalism*, Vintage Books – Random House, New York, 1976

Sterne, Laurence, *Tristram Shandy*, edited by Howard Anderson, W. W. Norton and Co., New York and London, 1980

Stevenson, Robert Louis, *Dr. Jekyll and Mr. Hyde*, Bantam Books, New York, London, Toronto, 1967

Svevo, Italo, *Confessions of Zeno*, translated by Beryl De Zoete, Vintage Books – Random House, New York, 1958

Thucydides, *The Landmark Thucydides, A Comprehensive Guide to the Peloponnesian War*, edited by Robert B. Strassler, The Free Press, New York, London, Toronto etc., 1996

Tolstoy, Leo, "The Death of Ivan Ilyich" in *Great Short Works of Leo Tolstoy*, Introduction John Bayley, translated by Louise and Aylmer Maude, Harper and Row, Publishers, New York, 1967

Trilling, Lionel, *The Moral Obligation to Be Intelligent, Selected Essays*, edited and Introduction by Leon Wieseltier, Farrar, Straus Giroux, New York, 2001

Unamuno, Miguel de, *Tragic Sense of Life*, translated by J. E. Crawford Flitch, Introduction by De Madariaga, Dover Publications, Inc., New York, 1954

Virgil, *The Aeneid*, translated by Robert Fitzgerald with Afterward, Vintage Classics – Random House, New York, 1990

Weil, Simone, "*The Iliad*, Poem of Might" in *Simone Weil Reader*, edited and Introduction by George A. Panichas, Moyer Bell Limited, Mt. Kisco, New York, 1977

Wilde, Oscar, "The Decay of Lying" and "Intentions" in *The Artist As Critic, Critical Writings of Oscar Wilde*, edited and Introduction by Richard Ellmann, University of Chicago Press, Chicago 1968, 1969

Wordsworth, William, *Supplementary to Preface of 1815 Lyrical Ballads*

Zeitlin, Irving, *Plato's Vision, The Classical Origin of Social and Political Thought*, Prentice Hall, Edgewood Cliffs, NJ, 1993

Printed in the United States
50899LVS00002B/877-945